The Art of Being Married

by

Rubel Shelly

20th CENTURY CHRISTIAN
2809 Granny White Pike
Nashville, Tennessee 37204

To

Myra

my companion-artist

Table of Contents

Foreword

When the most widely discussed subject is expounded by one of the most widely read Christian authors of the '80s, you have a magnificent combination! Thus, *The Art of Being Married*, by Dr. Rubel Shelly, brings together another lovely "marriage "

You've grown weary of hearing the problem cited, haven't you: one out of two marriages ends in divorce. Those that haven't split are fractured. Vows are lightly regarded; one couple wrote their own vows saying they would remain together "as long as we both do love"! Now comes a solution. Don't tell me the problem unless you can offer me tangible help in solving it.

In twelve chapters this God-fearing, truth-honoring, home-loving man does just this.

Dr. Shelly leads in vital chapters that will help everyone not just stay married but love "the assignment." Preparation, character, communication, intimacy, children, pitfalls are parts of this needed book.

So, by "popular request" according to an old statement and by timely emergencies to be met, we welcome this sensitive volume that has one aim: skill you in the "art of being married." We commend it to you.

Jim Bill McInteer

Introduction

Surprise! The family is alive and well in America today. Reports of its untimely demise were, apparently, grossly exaggerated.

A recent national poll taken by *USA Today*[1] reflected the statistic that nearly 80 percent of the married people questioned described their marriages as "warm and loving." Thirteen percent said marriage was for them a "peaceful coexistence" with their partners. Only six percent confessed to having serious marital problems.

While all of us welcome this resurgence of hope for the family, we realize that many who consider their present relationship a good one may soon face some intense stress that will cause it to fall apart. People really don't know how strong their marriages are until they face a great financial, emotional, or spiritual crisis.

Still others who are personally satisfied with their marriages may be unaware that God could be displeased with their arrangement. Some people are building on a foundation other than Jesus Christ and by a blueprint very different from the one found in the Word of God.

A friend of mine recently commented: "You know, there's a real art to this business of being married!" How right he is – and what a great idea for a book title. Beginning with his idea of marriage as an art form, I have tried to pull together some practical counsel about fashioning such a work of art in this book.

The Art of Being Married assumes that it is not getting married that is difficult but staying (i.e., being) married which is the real accomplishment. More than that, the staying together I have in mind is more than a grit-your-teeth situation of endurance; it is a relationship of love, confidence, and mutual growth.

This book builds around the motif of *seasons* (i.e., stages, identifiable periods) in marriage. Thus it begins with the initial decision about marriage, proceeds to discuss the importance of early adjustments in marriage, looks to the arrival of children, considers the possibility of problems so severe as to raise the option of divorce, and closes by looking at the role of grandparents. It can be studied with profit by any age group from high school students through senior citizens. A Teacher's Guide is available for it.

My special thanks go to Arnelle Adcock and Nancy Bennett for the research and writing they did for me on topics included in Chapters Nine, Ten, and Twelve. Their initial work was used for a series of five-minute radio programs and has been used freely in these three sections of this book.

Amy Jones has served as my secretary for several years and becomes increasingly important to my writing ministry as time goes by. She not only transcribes, edits, proofreads, and prepares the final manuscripts for all my writing projects but also keeps track of which one is due next – a task of no small proportion in my hectic schedule.

Above all, I thank God for the personal experience I have had in the context of my own marriage. My wife, Myra, and our three children have taught me the existential meaning of love, happiness, and peace. They have put the color, depth, and beauty on the canvas God gave me to paint in one lifetime.

1/ It's Not for Everybody

Nine out of every ten people who pick up this book are, or oneday will be, married.

Practically all of us feel a need for the intimate companionship of a person of the opposite sex in the context of commitment. People who do not believe in God explain that need as fundamentally biological and directly related to the need of our species to reproduce. People who think in theistic and biblical terms explain it in relation to the will of God in creating the human race.

God made it clear from the beginning that humans were being created as social entities in need of companionship. Having created the male of the species first, Yahweh said, "It is not good for the man to be alone. I will make a helper suitable for him" (Gen. 2:18).[1] A female was made whom Adam recognized as "bone of my bones and flesh of my flesh" (Gen. 2:23). Adam and Eve were brought together, united in marriage, and taught to hold fast to one another in commitment.

Occasionally one hears dire predictions about the survival of marriage as an institution. For example: "The family in its old sense is disappearing from our land, and not only our free institutions are threatened, but the very existence of our society is endangered." One gets the feeling that perhaps there is a bit of "crying wolf" in this statement

1

when he realizes it was made in the *Boston Quarterly Review* of 1859.

Marxism has decried marriage as sexual exploitation. Radical feminists had some very negative things to say about marriage and its ability to survive. Futurists of a couple of decades ago assured us that serial monogamy (i.e., short-term commitment) was the coming thing and traditional marriage was on the way out.

That 90 percent of all people eventually marry indicates that the heterosexual arrangement we call "traditional marriage" remains the norm for our society. Practical experience has validated the biblical statement: "He who finds a wife finds what is good and receives favor from the Lord" (Prov. 18:22).

Some Will Not Marry

There are some people, however, who *do not* marry. A relatively small percentage of these people will never have the opportunity to marry. Most of them will forego marriage by choice. Indeed, there are some people who *should not* get married.

Although the Bible acknowledges married life as the norm, it imposes no obligation on anyone to marry and have a family. Jesus was not married, and he said some would choose not to marry "for the kingdom of heaven's sake" (Matt. 19:12). Neither did the apostle Paul head a family unit.[2] He called the single life a "gift of God" to certain individuals (1 Cor. 7:7).

The number of people who choose *never* to marry has increased significantly in this century. From 1970 to 1982, the Census Bureau reports that this element of U.S. population grew 115 percent to six million men and women – with just slightly more women than men in the group.

Many factors contribute to explaining this phenomenon. **Societal attitudes** certainly make the single life easier for many. The pressure to conform by getting married is not as strong as it once was. People are no longer regarded as abnormal for not marrying. The women's movement has certainly had some impact as well. More women are pursuing professions and following options open to them as single persons which were not there only a few years ago. It is estimated, for example, that the number of women earning college degrees in business will be eight times as great in 1990 as it was in the 1960s.

Economics has played a role in helping some people decide against marriage. It just isn't true that "two can live as cheaply as one," and some people realize and accept that fact. Unable in their judgment to handle the financial responsibility of a mate and children, some decide not to marry. Some choose careers where being single gives special opportunities. It is certainly easier to pick up and move when there are not other persons to take into account.

Some people simply say they like the **freedom and flexibility** of going solo. A friend of mine did not make an early decision against marriage. But he did commit to a long process of education and a demanding career. In his mid-thirties, he had developed a lifestyle which he enjoyed too much to consider giving up for marriage. He's no "swinger" or selfish person. He just built a pattern of living, working, traveling, and befriending which he found satisfying without marriage. He certainly does not give the impression of being frustrated or unhappy with his decision. A wife and three children have been God's gift to me; a single life has been God's gift to Don.

Affluence makes it possible. Many businesses cater to it. Society does a better job of accepting it than in days gone by. The single life is a reality for about 12 percent of our contemporaries.

Other One-Adult Households

An even larger percentage of the total population is living the single life perhaps only temporarily. This group would include young adults who are still single but will oneday get married, divorced persons, widows, and widowers. Among the nation's 20- to 44-year-olds, 38 percent (approximately 34 million people) were single at the beginning of 1985 –almost twice as many as a decade ago.

The "traditional American family" (i.e., father as breadwinner, mother as homemaker, and children) is largely a myth now, since a distinct minority of only seven percent of America's population fits that profile. There is a healthy appreciation for such units, but their existence is increasingly rare.

New models of life patterns are emerging where single persons and single-parent families will be more in evidence. A report by demographers at the Joint Center for Urban Studies of MIT and Harvard, entitled "The Nation's Families 1960-1990," made several predictions for 1990. Among them were the following: (1) at least 13 separate types of households will eclipse the conventional family, including such categories as "female head, widowed, with children" and "male head, previously married, with children," (2) more than a third of the couples first married in the 1970s will have divorced, and (3) more than a third of the children born in the 1970s will have spent part of their childhood living with a single parent.[3]

The median age for a first marriage in the United States has increased two full years since 1970 – from 23.2 to 25.4 for men and from 20.8 to 22.8 for women.[4] This statistic has both good and bad implications. On the positive side, it is good for people to be genuine adults before getting married; the highest incidence of marital failure is among people who marry while still in their teens or immediately after high school. On the negative side, physical maturity and unrestricted social freedom can create intense temptations to sexual sin; Paul faced up to this very realistic situation in 1 Corinthians 7:9.

As of 1983, there were 114 divorced people for every 1,000 married ones in the United States. Many of these will eventually marry again, but they are one-adult households for the time being.

Even more widows and widowers live alone than divorced persons. Just at 13 percent of the adult population of America is in this category.

Put this group with those who choose never to marry and those broken (but not divorced) family units in our society and the fact emerges that "one in five U.S. households now consists of only one member."[5]

4

The much-publicized modern arrangement of "persons of the opposite sex sharing living quarters" is the lifestyle of only about three to four percent of our total population. Researchers from many fields other than religion and Christian ethics have challenged the myth that living together is a satisfying alternative to marriage.

From this perspective, it is clear that living together is a denial and avoidance of the profound religious, political, legal, and sociocultural meanings and values of marriage. A viable human society is inextricably linked to a viable marital and family structure.[6]

Living together is not a satisfying alternative to marriage, and it will not replace marriage as the norm for stable interpersonal relationships.

As a recent major newspaper survey indicates, Americans still cherish the idea of a family. Most people want the benefits that come of a stable marriage.[7]

The focus of attention needs to be where the people are: the majority of us who live in traditional marriage arrangements and the second-largest group which is living the single life –whether temporarily or permanently.

This book is going to focus on *the art of being married* and will not attempt to deal at great length with many of the problems and challenges of being single – whether temporarily or permanently. Even most of what will be said to singles will be to those who are looking toward and preparing for marriage. But there are a few things about singleness which ought to be said at this point.

Some OUGHT To Stay Single

When Paul wrote to the church at Corinth, he never inveighed against marriage for single or widowed persons – though he did make it clear that some divorced people could not marry a second time with God's approval (cf. 1 Cor. 7:10-11). On the other hand, he *recommended* single-ness to unmarried saints in that city. There was apparently some crisis situation facing the church there (1 Cor. 7:26) which made any change in lifestyle a special challenge at the time. That situation aside, however, he had some things to say about the advantages of being single which don't receive a great deal of emphasis in our teaching.

Singleness isn't a disease, and those who are married need not feel either superior to unmarrieds or compelled to dabble in matchmaking. Single people should not be left out of the life of the church or the personal lives of couples and families with children.

First, some persons ought to forego marriage – at least temporarily – because of certain career ambitions they have embraced.

This seems to have been Paul's thinking in his personal decision about staying single. "But I would have you to be free from cares. He that is unmarried is careful for the things of the Lord, how he may please the Lord: but he that is married is careful for the things of the world, how he may please his wife, and is divided" (1 Cor. 7:32-34a).

Even in his pre-conversion life, he appears to have been consumed by his work within Judaism. Then, when he became a Christian, he gave his entire life to travel and work in trying to establish the church throughout the Roman Empire of his time. Concern for his own health and safety were often set aside for the sake of a perilous mission. It would have been irresponsible to disregard those same factors if a wife and children had been involved. One can make personal sacrifices for the sake of a work he is committed to performing which he has no right to impose unilaterally on others under his authority.

I fear that I have known some preachers, missionaries, and church workers who should have stayed single. They got married, however, and then neglected the emotional and spiritual needs of their own families for the sake of serving others. It is not the sincerity or dedication of these men that is in question. It is their judgment, sense of fairness with the people to whom they owed more than any others, and ability to handle multiple responsibilities with a proper sense of priority.

The same mistake has been made by men who are in medicine, accounting, law, groceries, or farming. If one chooses to have a family, the family and its needs must come before career ambition and second only to God. As surely as John could say that one who claims to love God but mistreats his brother is a liar (1 John 4:20), one could – with even greater justification – make the same charge about one who claims to love God while neglecting or otherwise mistreating his/her family. If it comes to the choice of sacrificing one to the other, the career ambition must be laid aside for the sake of the family responsibility.

Some women have tried to weld demanding personal careers with being wives and mothers – only to learn that one or the other has to be compromised for the sake of the other. In 1985 more than six of 10 mothers with children under 18 are in the public work force; this figure is up nearly 45 percent from 1970. Sometimes success in the career has been so important that it was the family responsibility which was sacrificed.

Now please don't misunderstand what is being said here. It is not wrong for either a man or a woman to commit to a demanding career and marriage, too. Some people can handle it. But some can't. One needs to be completely honest in making the decision. And both partners will need to understand what is being committed to and what will be asked by way of personal sacrifice. If either does not agree that the sacrifices are worthwhile for the goal in view, the couple should not marry.

Second, an individual for whom personal freedom is all important ought not get married.

Can you give up whatever you have worked (or are working) to attain, if the marriage demands it? If you can't give an honest "yes" to this question, you should not get married.

If a woman is so fiercely independent that the thought of agreeing to "love, honor, and *obey*" is galling, she shouldn't get married. In the marriage relationship, it will be her spiritual responsibility to defer to her husband as the final decision-maker for the family. If being "tied down" is more than you could live with, marriage just isn't for you.

Personal freedom has to be sacrificed for the sake of

the other person in marriage. Nothing will so surely doom a marriage to failure as one person's inability to sacrifice what he or she wants (and could have if single!) for the sake of something the family unit needs. If your disposition doesn't allow that sort of self-denial, admit it. Don't make the mistake of thinking you can marry and be the independent person you have been to this point in your life. This caution needs to be taken especially seriously the older you are. You have made some pretty deep ruts in life's road by now, and it may be too difficult to get out of them for the sake of getting married. If so, don't!

A girl who grew up in the context of a home environment where the father mistreated her mother was determined never to be dependent on any man. She did, however, decide to marry. She kept her maiden name after the wedding, continued to work and keep her income separate from her husband's, and occasionally took a trip alone to emphasize that her life was not going to be subservient to her husband's. As she put it, she set about a course of "preserving her independent identity" from the man she married. The marriage lasted less than two years.

The married life is one of *inter*dependence rather than *in*dependence. The man or woman who cannot subject himself/herself to his/her partner in the relationship should commit to the single life.

Third, if there is some obstacle between two people which they have been unable to deal with during their courtship, they should be wise enough not to get married (cf. Eph. 5:21).

Any problem can be handled by two people willing to work together in respect and love for each other. In-laws, money, career – anything can be handled so long as the two people are committed to each other in genuine love.

Suppose, however, there is some problem which has nagged two people all during their courtship. It has been a frequent source of tension, and finally they just get to the point where the issue is totally avoided. They are about to get married in the unrealistic expectation that it will somehow "take care of itself" after the wedding day. That is a foolish mistake. If the matter cannot be negotiated and resolved during courtship, chances are it will destroy the marriage later. There is a fate far worse than calling off a wedding. And that worse fate is marrying unrealistically and reaping the constant fruit of tension and bitterness in the marriage –if it holds together at all.

The problem can be one of an almost endless list. One which causes frequent difficulties is conflict over religion. One whose faith is personal, intelligent, and deep will want to share it with the individual whose life is most intimately connected with his.

Edward was Catholic, and Judy could hardly bring up the subject of religion without casting a chill over their relationship. For a while, they went their separate ways on Sundays and continued to date. She even accepted a ring and set a wedding date nearly a year away. But she began observing couples whose home was divided along lines of faith. She saw women less involved in the work of the church than she wanted to be. She saw children pulled first one way and then the other by their parents. She even noticed that the teen-aged children of some divided couples were totally non-religious and suspected some relationship between their total rejection of faith and the confusion they had experienced in their homes.

Judy insisted that she and Edward face their differences. They met with both a preacher and a priest. They talked privately. It became apparent that the situation was one of impasse. As difficult as it was to make the decision, she broke the engagement. Her mature assessment was that the grief of a broken engagement would be far less than the grief of a religiously mixed marriage.

While it is not sinful to marry a non-Christian (cf. 1 Cor. 7:12-14; 1 Pet. 3:1-2), it will be a less-than-ideal relationship.

Fourth, people who are emotionally, financially, or otherwise unable to assume the responsibility for another person's happiness and well-being should not marry.

Maturity is a hard thing to measure. It is not always directly related to chronological age. Some people never grow up! They do not have a clear sense of purpose for their lives. They cannot accept responsibility for their mistakes and deal with problems realistically. They will not admit it when wrong or make the changes in thinking and behavior which go with maturity. They cannot think for themselves and are always blown about by whichever wind is stronger at the moment.

Immature persons go into panic whenever any crisis situation arises. They cannot save money or manage debts responsibly. They have few intelligent convictions but a host of dogmatic prejudices. They have unhealthy attitudes toward sex. They are generally disorganized and lacking in self-discipline. They are unable to deny their self-interests for the sake of others.

Everyone acts with varying levels of maturity in different situations. The point here is not that one must be totally competent and poised under every conceivable circumstance to be considered a mature adult. On balance, however, one must be able to point to a pattern of behavior that is appropriate and constructive in dealing with life.

The unfortunate thing about immaturity is that it is blind to itself. This means that it is terribly naive to expect immature people to decide against marriage on the basis of their immaturity. On the other hand, a mature person who is considering the commitment of marriage with someone who exhibits quite a few of the traits of immaturity listed above should put off the wedding until the other person grows up a bit. If he or she doesn't grow up, that person should be smart enough not to get into the boat of matrimony with someone who will be rocking it constantly.

Conclusion

Marriage just isn't the right answer for everyone. Maybe our society is beginning to see and accept that fact. Perhaps this means that fewer people will be getting married just because "it's the thing to do." This, we can hope, will mean more people getting married because they are really in love, making commitments that harbor no reservations, and producing more genuinely successful homes.

For those who are single, many churches have developed special ministries. Christian singles who see their situation as one of trauma and loneliness rather than choice need the spiritual family of God to step in to provide support and strength. For those who have gone through the pain of divorce or the death of a mate, the church must mediate grace and healing in Jesus' name. The body of Christ must reach out and embrace people living the single life – whether doing so permanently or temporarily.

At the same time, ministries to single adults must not be condescending. Singleness is the status of choice rather than necessity for many people. They are not social or emotional misfits; they are not takers as opposed to givers. They have skills, interests, and outlets that allow them to be useful leaders in the life of the church.

2/ Marriage:
Most Will Try

Wedding bells continue to ring!

A study done by the Institute of Social Research at the University of Michigan at the start of this decade revealed that only three percent of the 18-year-olds questioned thought they would not marry. An insurance industry survey released in 1983 found that 85 percent of single persons in this country would prefer to be married. In fact, approximately 90 percent of the population of America *will* marry.

The divorce rate is high. There were two and one-half million marriages in America last year; there were one and one-quarter million divorces. But it isn't frightening off too many people that a lot of their peers are failing. They think they can marry and make it work. They are determined.

Sociological studies support the claim that more people are taking their marriages seriously and are committed to making them work. Although the divorce rate increased by 113 percent in the 1970s, it has slowed significantly in the 1980s. Through the first three years of the present decade, the divorce rate has gone up only about 14 percent.[1]

Some of the mind-molding media of the Western world seem intent on giving a negative picture of marriage. Adulterous affairs are presented sympathetically in movies and

TV dramas. Judith Crist is a nationally known film commentator and has said:

> I consider movies a reflection of contemporary morality. I'm not saying everyone should clear their sinuses by having an affair. But I personally feel that today's morality is better for its pure notion that going to bed with someone else, that's no reason to give up your home and children. It's healthy.[2]

In the typical situation comedy, husbands and fathers are bumblers who have to be rescued from their stupidity by their astute children; mothers are mindless morons who keep us in stitches with their silly schemes which always fail. People apparently haven't been convinced, for they are willing to take the plunge into matrimony seriously.

To be sure, marriages today have quite a different look than they did 50 years ago. Dual-career marriages are no longer unusual. More and more people are willing to challenge traditional barriers and to marry across economic, cultural, and racial lines. With higher educational backgrounds and in a generally affluent culture, people are postponing marriage a few years longer than they once did. When they do marry, however, they expect a great deal of the relationship.

Marriage is a God-ordained relationship between two persons. It holds unlimited opportunities and imposes serious responsibilities. More of us need to understand exactly *what* it is and *why* we choose it over other alternatives for our lives.

What Is Marriage?

Here is a simple and biblical definition of marriage: *it is a formal promise between a man and woman which makes of them (and any children they bring into their home) a family.*

First, it is a promise-based relationship. The word used throughout Scripture to refer to promise-bounded situations is *covenant* (Heb, *berith*; Gk, *diatheke*).

In rebuking certain marriages Israelite men had made with pagan women, the prophet Malachi wrote:

You weep and wail because [the Lord] no longer pays attention to your offerings or accepts them with pleasure from your hands. You ask, "Why?" It is because the Lord is acting as the witness between you and the wife of your youth, because you have broken faith with her, though she is your partner, the wife of your marriage covenant. Has not the Lord made them one? In flesh and spirit they are his. And why one? Because he was seeking godly offspring. So guard yourself in your spirit, and do not break faith with the wife of your youth (Mal. 2:13b-15).

In describing Judah as an unfaithful wife, God used the covenant principle as an expression of the essence of that relationship. "I gave you my solemn oath (plighted my troth to you, RSV) and entered into a covenant with you, declares the Sovereign Lord, and you became mine" (Ezek. 16:8b). But she violated the covenant to "commit adultery" with her idolatrous neighbors. Thus Judah was to be judged: "I will sentence you to the punishment of women who commit adultery and who shed blood; I will bring upon you the blood vengeance of my wrath and jealous anger" (Ezek. 16:38). In her sin, she had "despised my oath by breaking the covenant" (Ezek. 16:59).

Although covenants are of different types in Scripture, the basic feature of them all is a contractual (i.e., promise-bounded) relationship involving mutual privileges and responsibilities.

When we *make* and *keep* promises, we are acting in likeness to our promise-making and promise-keeping God. It is the only way to take unbearable uncertainty out of the future. G. K. Chesterton said, "The person who makes a vow makes an appointment with himself at some distant time or place." Our ability to depend on one another to keep those appointments is the basis for most of the meaningful things we do in life.

Why would Abraham leave Chaldean security for a never-before-seen land? He trusted God's promise to him. Why did Moses undertake to lead two million or more ill-equipped Hebrews out of Egypt? He believed God's promise made to him out in the desert. Why do we have confidence of the new heaven and new earth? We believe God's promise.

Why does Helen commit to marry Steve? She believes that Steve means it when he says he will love her, be faithful to her, and provide for her happiness until death separates them. She believes his promise and is willing to respond by making the same one to him.

Lewis Smedes speaks of the "paradox of promising." It is an act in which one freely binds himself to give up his freedom for the sake of keeping his word on some matter. "We limit our freedom," he says, "so that we can be free to be there with someone in his future's unpredictable storms."

Second, marriage is a formal commitment which has been solemnized before God and men by making the promise a matter of public record.

This is to say that a man and woman are not married simply because they have pledged their love and promised to stay together for life. People make such pledges thoughtlessly at times or in the fervor of passion. Unless the requirements of civil law concerning a marriage license, duly authorized officiant, and so forth are complied with, a marriage does not exist between two people.

Since the power of the state to regulate marriage is from God (Rom. 13:1ff), failure to acknowledge and submit to its authority nullifies the legitimacy of the union. Christians must "be subject to every ordinance of man for the Lord's sake" (1 Pet. 2:13a).

Even sexual union with another person does not constitute marriage apart from the formal making of a covenant between them. Under the Law of Moses, a man who had sexual relations with a virgin was honor bound to marry her; even so, her father could refuse to allow the marriage to take place (Ex. 22:16-17). Since marriage was something which followed on the fact of their sexual union, marriage is obviously something distinct from sexual contact.

From the New Testament we learn that sex is a privilege reserved for those who have already made the formal covenant which constitutes marriage (Heb. 13:4). And while it is true that one can become "one flesh" with a prostitute by joining his body with hers (cf. 1 Cor. 6:16), that sort of union is fornication –not marriage.

The practical justification for courtship, engagement, announcement of a wedding date, and the legal demands surrounding marriage is two-fold: (1) it encourages the couple to enter the relationship thoughtfully and deliberately and (2) it announces to the world their honorable intention to live together under the laws and customs of their society.

God's laws concerning marriage have priority, of course, over the laws of men. There are no marriages recognized by God which have not been legitimized under the laws and mores of a given society. On the other hand, a given society may honor some unions as marriage (e.g., homosexual "marriages," cf. Matt. 19:9; 1 Cor. 7:10-11) which God has not authorized and thus does not recognize.

Third, the formalization of such a promise between two eligible persons constitutes them (and any children who may result from their union) a family.

Practically everyone recognizes the family as the basic organizational structure of all society. The reason society at large is in such jeopardy is because the glue which holds all human relationships intact is in short supply in family units. That "glue" is fidelity to promises.

Do you ever feel frustrated that treaties and international agreements are so fragile as to be generally worthless? Does it bother you that politicians make campaign pledges which are never honored? Have guarantees, warranties, and contracts become less meaningful in your experience? Perhaps it traces to the fact that so many people have learned in their families that promises don't have to be kept and therefore have no misgivings over breaking other pledges and vows. Thinking back to Chapter One again, the inability of immature persons to make and keep promises is why they are unsuitable for marriage.

Harry is a Christian man whose wife was unfaithful to him. She had an affair which lasted for several months.

17

When it came to light, his heart was broken. "I promised to love her until death," he told me, "and I will forgive her and take her back. I'll do everything I can to help her and put our marriage back together." There is a man whose word means something! Even after his wife broke her promise to him, he was willing to keep his end of the bargain. (Shades of how God treats us!) There is no circumstance on earth – whether regarding land, money, or really important things – in which I would doubt Harry's promise to me about anything. I know he makes his word good.

Somewhere today there is a man's whose son is in trouble with the law again. Whatever inclination he has to say "I wish he'd just leave and never show his face in this house again" is stifled for the sake of a promise he made to God when that child was born, and he keeps on loving in the context of pain and trying to help. Somewhere there is a woman who is thinking to herself, "No one knows how miserably unhappy I am with this boorish husband of mine. Surely I could divorce him and do better." But she won't divorce him. She made a promise to him, and she will keep it.

The heart of everything that has to do with marriage and family revolves around making and keeping promises. The very nature of marriage centers on this phenomenon.

Why People Marry

As risky as it is to make promises about a future which cannot be foreseen, we remain willing to take the gamble. We remain willing to stand before God and men to pledge our fidelity to one another.

When one stops to think what a momentous thing it is, he may wonder why everyone doesn't just declare for the single life and spare himself the potential challenge – even sacrifice and grief – which such a promise can entail. Why *do* we keep on opting for marriage?

1. God created humans with a fundamental need for companionship.

To be *alone* is not necessarily to be *lonely*. Some people prefer to live in isolation. Others are content with superficial relationships with men and women in their environment. Still other persons establish close and firm friendships which meet their need for companionship without marriage. The way most of us choose to meet our deepest need for human companionship is through marriage.

A network television special dealing with the single life cited what one single person called "a plague of loneliness and isolation" in his life. Despite the clubs, dating services, and singles gatherings in various contexts, many unmarried persons of the baby boom generation are longing for the intimate companionship of marriage. As reporter Jack Reynolds said in closing the program: "For many people, particularly women, being single seems to have turned out to be more complicated and less fun than they'd assumed. ... [T]he great American disease of this century is loneliness, and the 'baby boom generation' is rediscovering that a good marriage is one of the best cures."[3]

God made us male and female. "And God created man (i.e., mankind, human beings) in his own image, in the image of God created he him; male and female created he them" (Gen. 1:27). Adam was created before Eve, and every form of animal life was brought before him to name (Gen. 1:19). The purpose of this seems to have been to impress the man with what God already knew about him: he needed someone like him as a companion, helper, and mate (cf. Gen. 1:18, 20). When Eve was created and brought to him, Adam rejoiced that his loneliness was over (Gen. 1:23).

Health studies have long pointed to the fact that single, widowed, and divorced persons are far likelier to be victims of serious disease than married folk. The coronary death rate among widows between 25 and 34 is five times that of married women in the same age group. Among divorced white males, cirrhosis of the liver is seven times more common and tuberculosis ten times more frequent. At all ages among both males and females, the divorced are twice as likely as the married to develop lung cancer or suffer a stroke. Psychologist James J. Lynch wrote a book several years back entitled *The Broken Heart: The Medical Consequences of Loneliness.* "Loneliness," he said, "is pushing our physical health to the breaking point."

Each of us needs someone with whom to share joys and

sorrows (Rom. 12:15). We need someone to back us and help us in troubled times (Gal. 6:2). Sure, we need occasional periods of being alone and "having some space." But the greatest moments of our lives are those *shared* events of love, compassion, and joy. These are the times we cannot do without. Our physical, emotional, and spiritual health depend on them.

The combined experience of the human race says that marriage is the best place to find intimate companionship. Males and females are drawn to each other, pair off because they find themselves complemented and fulfilled in one another, and marry.

2. We need the security of love within the context of commitment.

About three percent of the American population is made up of persons of the opposite sex living together without benefit of wedlock. Several sociologists have expressed the concern that living together as a substitute for marriage reflects an unhealthy trait. The inability or unwillingness of people to make permanent commitments is taking away a crucial element of their humanness, of their ability to live responsibly in society.

Remember what was said earlier about marriage as a "promise-based relationship"? Psychologist Urie Bronfenbrenner has expressed the view that cohabitation as a substitute for marriage undermines the sense of obligation in all love and work relationships. "Society needs some kind of custom or institution in which people are committed to each other, no matter what," he says. "In sleeping together you don't develop those commitments."

Glen Campbell extolled in song the state of unmarried cohabitation as one to be preferred over marriage. He opined that living with a woman while keeping his bedroll stashed behind the couch was better than being shackled by ink stains on a marriage license. That arrangement, he told his bedmate, "keeps you ever gentle on my mind." What such an arrangement really does, we have found out, is free him of responsibility and leave him ready to run at the first sign of a difficulty.

Marriage is a long-range commitment of love and involves an implicit agreement to work through whatever challenges to that relationship which may arise. Living together without marriage is an irresponsible way – especially for the male of the species – to secure a sex partner for the time being and say "I'm splitting" when a problem comes. We need more personal security than such a relationship can possibly provide.

3. Marriage is where our need for sexual gratification can be satisfied in harmony with the will of God.

The Bible has a positive attitude toward human sexuality. The one-flesh nature of marriage has been emphasized from Eden forward (cf. Gen. 2:24-25). Sexual attraction is often the first thing which draws a given individual to another. He finds her beautiful and can't stop thinking about her; she thinks he's better looking than Tom Selleck. Then, as they date and their initial attraction begins maturing into love, another level of sexual desire begins to emerge. A sense of passionate desire for one another prompts them to express their love through embracing, kissing, and the desire for total sharing of their bodies. That is normal, healthy, and right.

If these desires are right, then why is their satisfaction wrong before marriage? Sex is not for halfway commitments.

Two people sharing their bodies in bed is beautiful when that sharing is the celebration of their total commitment to each other as companions in the security of pledged love. This is why a wedding should be such a joyous event. It is both a solemn exchanging of vows and a party atmosphere where two people under God proclaim to the world an all-or-nothing commitment of their lives to each other. In that context, sex is appropriate. Oh, it still brings a certain pleasure without the wedding and when shared in secrecy. But things have a characteristic way of going wrong quickly when sex is taken from its natural and God-ordained place and misused.

Almost every couple having sex during their courtship says, "We're different, though. We will stay together. Sex isn't a one-night stand for us. It is our enjoyment of each other and a deepening of our level of commitment prior to marriage." The odds aren't terribly good that a couple will stay together through courtship into marriage. If you think the divorce rate is high, how high do you think the break-up rate is?

Tim Stafford has put it very well in these words:

> You've gone "all the way" physically, but haven't gone "all the way" in commitment. The two should be synchronized, but they aren't in your case. Consequently your love can't grow through the daily sharing of married life. Under such circumstances your relationship can begin to act like a car that has its timing off – starting and bucking and stopping, because all the parts aren't working together.[4]

Humans want and need sexual gratification. The Christian accepts the fact that marriage is the only legitimate arrangement which allows for it. He or she heeds the inspired counsel of Paul to the effect that the choice is between self-discipline in sexual feelings or marriage. There is no moral right to opt for a third course of all-the-way sex during courtship. "But if they cannot control themselves, they should marry, for it is better to marry than to burn with passion" (1 Cor. 7:9).

4. Every human being needs a place of unconditional acceptance, and marriage is God's answer to that need.

Let's get back to the business of promise and commitment for a moment. In marriage, two persons voluntarily commit themselves to each other for life. Accepting what we have chosen, we love despite whatever imperfections we may subsequently discover. After all, God loves us despite our imperfections. God doesn't quit loving us because we are imperfect; his example is the one we are trying to imitate in relation to one another in marriage.

Some of us are moody. All of us have things happen to our health, careers, or life ambitions. Everyone needs to be respected for the good points he or she has and tolerated for his or her imperfections. Some people are even psychotic, alcoholic, or dangerous. As abominable as these things may be in another person, marriage is a commitment where one *promises* to remain faithful in sickness and in health, for better or for worse.

So many people marry expecting perfection of their partners that it is no wonder when they rush to the divorce courts. There is no such thing as a perfect person, a perfect husband, a perfect wife. In realistic and mature Christian marriage, we accept and live with that fact.

We have something of a model of how marriage should work when we think of the relationship between parents and children. If mom and dad have problems with a teenager, they can't send him back to the womb for a fresh start. Neither can they just call off the matter of their responsibility to him and "wash their hands" of him. On the other hands, the teen-aged son is stuck with the parents he got. They may not be wise, prosperous, or famous, but they are his parents. In the same way, a husband and wife are one flesh in their relationship.

With an even deeper commitment to one another than that which exists naturally between parent and child, a husband and wife belong to one another (Gen. 2:24). To quit on that commitment and to divorce one's husband or wife is like cutting off a part of one's own body (Eph. 5:28-30).

No one really knows the person he or she marries until the marriage has been functioning for a while. During courtship, each is on his best behavior. Bad moods can be masked. Resentments can be stifled. Little irritations can be tolerated. After all, these people spend only a few hours together during the week and can regroup during their time apart. After the wedding, however, it is a different matter. You are together every day – on the bad ones as well as the good ones. You are rubbing elbows on everything from eating habits to job pressures to serious illness. Each of us enters marriage expecting to be accepted in all these things. It is only right to extend that same acceptance to the other person.

The Son of God shows us that love is a free and undeserved gift. We cannot love only when our mates deserve love. If anything, we must love all the more when they are undeserving.

5. Everyone needs someone to make happy.

With only occasional exceptions, marriage is the result of a process which runs this course: Alice sees and is attracted to Bob, Alice seeks for ways to get Bob's attention by lavishing attention on and making Bob happy, Bob starts looking for ways to return joy and happiness to Alice, and finally Alice and Bob decide they want to spend the rest of their lives performing this happiness function for each other.

If this pattern continues after the wedding, the marriage will be successful. Unfortunately, however, it sometimes breaks down shortly after the commitment to wedlock is made. For some strange reason, Alice and Bob may stop thinking about *giving* happiness and start concentrating on *getting* it. Frustration is inevitable. Love, joy, and peace are things that can be received only through giving in kind.

Take Alice and her housework, for example. In spite of all the changes that have taken place in thinking about marital roles, women are generally still responsible for maintaining the smooth functioning of the house. In the beginning of the marriage, Bob was probably very thoughtful of Alice. He helped her make the bed in the morning, dried when she washed, took out the garbage, etc. Those times may have provided some powerful bonding experiences of casual conversation, shared duties, and little courtesies. As Bob begins to neglect these things, Alice may begin feeling victimized, unappreciated, and used.

Or consider Bob and their sex life. On the honeymoon and for some time thereafter, he was tender, patient, and concerned that the experience be one of joy for Alice. After a while, however, he can begin being thoughtless of her, have what he wants, and leave her lying awake frustrated and crying as he drifts off to sleep.

The uniquely Christian word for love in Scripture is *agape*. The word refers to self-giving concern for another. It is not selfish. It does not take advantage of another. It is always looking to give rather than get. This is the kind of love which good marriages must have for a foundation.

In the long run, it is in one's personal self-interest to love selflessly. Making someone else happy makes her happy. Giving joy to another person creates a sense of joy in his heart. Marriage is the best context for learning and exhibiting the sort of love that makes other people happy and, in turn, brings happiness to the giver.

Conclusion

Some things cannot be assigned a dollar value. Yet they are of great worth. They have their worth in terms of life, happiness, and fulfillment. Marriage is one of those things.

Because marriage provides companionship, the security of loving commitment, sexual gratification, acceptance, and personal happiness, people keep on seeking this relationship. They will as long as life continues on this planet.

3/ A Woman Prepares for Marriage

Where does one go in the Word of God to find the most direct and practical counsel for a woman who is thinking about marriage?

Allow me to suggest that we go to 1 Peter 3:1-6. Why these verses? They seem to be an excellent summary of the four fundamental traits of character which allow a woman to be a Christian wife. If these four traits are primary to building a good marriage, any woman would be wise to develop them before her wedding and to look for a man who both appreciates and complements them.

> Likewise you wives, be submissive to your husbands, so that some, though they do not obey the word, may be won without a word by the behavior of their wives, when they see your reverent and chaste behavior. Let not yours be the outward adorning with braiding of hair, decoration of gold, and wearing of fine clothing, but let it be the hidden person of the heart with the imperishable jewel of a gentle and quiet spirit, which in God's sight is very precious. So once the holy women who hoped in God used to adorn themselves and were submissive to their husbands, as Sarah obeyed Abraham, calling him lord. And you are now her children if you do right and let nothing terrify you (1 Pet. 3:1-6 RSV).

In their original context, these verses give counsel to Christian women who are married to non-Christian men. They focus on four traits which would enable many of those women to lead their mates to faith in Christ "without talk by the behavior of their wives" (NIV). Surely, then, these are the most important features of personality for any believing woman to develop. They are the ones which will give the individual married to a non-Christian the best chance to reach him; they will allow two Christians to reach the full potential for happiness and stability in their relationship.

Since we are thinking about *preparation* for marriage, our concern will be to find the personality traits which will bring about the achievement of these four goals within marriage.

Unselfishness

The first thing Peter talks about in this paragraph is a wife's **submission to her husband.** For one thing, these are almost fighting words to some elements of female society today. For another, one wonders how a woman who is willing to live in submission to a man can prepare herself for that role. If we understand what the Bible means by submission, the "sting" of the idea is removed and one sees quickly how a woman can prepare for this element of her marital responsibility.

A "traditionalist" view equates submission with subservience, loss of individuality, dependence, and unquestioning obedience. Leaders of the modern feminist movement openly express their hostility toward Christianity and its teaching about women, calling it "sexist" and "oppressive." What these people resent and oppose is not the Bible's teaching about women but the false interpretations of it by certain individuals and groups (i.e., the "traditionalists") and the ungodly fruits of oppression those interpretations have generated.

It is something like the history of civil rights for blacks in this country. The Bible never sanctioned slavery, compulsory segregation, or the denial of opportunity to blacks.

28

However, the Bible was used by racists to promote and defend these evils through the twisting and perverting of certain texts.

Similarly, the Bible has always upheld the dignity of woman and insisted on her fair treatment in every setting. Some people have wrested Scripture in an effort to degrade women and deny them equitable treatment in many situations.

What I have called the traditionalist view equates submission with inferiority. Written at a time when women generally were regarded as property and given no rights, the Scripture holds women in high regard and teaches that females of the race are due respect and dignity. Woman is as essential as man to the "image of God" in the human race (Gen. 1:27). Jesus' ministry included the presence, support, and service of women (Luke 8:1-3). There is equality of access into divine grace for males and females (Gal. 3:28). The role of women in relation to men in the affairs of the church and family is nowhere interpreted in the Bible as signifying her inferiority or lack of worth.

The Bible nowhere commands women to get married. They may pursue careers (e.g., Lydia, Acts 16:11-15) as single persons. In situations where a woman has chosen that life, she should be treated fairly, given an opportunity to do work for which she is qualified, and paid the same as a man who is doing an equivalent task and who has similar training and experience. This is just a practical application of the Golden Rule.

For a woman who chooses to marry, however, decision-making involves two persons. According to the will of God, she has submitted to the leadership of a man through her own free choice. She understands that any functioning entity has to have a center of authority and that God has ordained that the man fill that role in marriage. As she looks to the Lord Jesus, she finds a perfect model of willing submission to the Father. His submission never diminished his worth or personhood, yet it did cause him to say, "Not my will, but yours be done" (Luke 22:42).

An unmarried woman has options that a married person does not have. There are possibilities open to a married couple without children that are closed to a married couple with children. To the degree that any individual makes a commitment of self-giving love to another, that individual is implicitly giving up certain rights.

On the other hand, a married woman has options a single one does not have. She has an identity that is larger than herself. Her life has its meaning intertwined with that one someone whom she loves more than her own life. She is not dominated or tyrannized by that man. She is not in a constant tug-of-war with him over rights. She has unselfishly and voluntarily given herself over to him and his leadership. As the church is voluntarily in subjection to Christ, so she is in voluntary subjection to a man whom she trusts (cf. Eph. 5:22).

While still in the dating stage, a woman reveals her character as selfish or unselfish in nature.

Suppose she is so insecure that she must always be making absurd demands on a man. She wants gifts he cannot afford, makes him feel guilty for not being able to take her the places she wants to go, and otherwise shows herself unappreciative of his best efforts to make her happy. This pattern will not disappear after the marriage ceremony has been said.

Suppose she cannot understand when his boss demands that he work late on a Friday evening when they were supposed to go out. It becomes a major production and takes two or three weeks for her to quit pouting. She is showing herself to be a selfish stinker!

A selfish person is not a good marriage risk. She is not mature enough to put herself in subjection to her husband, to do without things she wants while they are still struggling to get on their financial feet, or to meet the demands that will be made by a crying or sick baby.

Purity

Second, Peter says that Christian women should be distinguished by their **purity** (i.e., chaste behavior).

Some segments of our society denigrate women in both obvious and subtle ways. In our sex-obsessed culture, women are routinely exploited as sex-objects – and the emphasis here should be on the word "objects." Clubs feature nude dancing girls or female mud wrestlers, movies throw in scenes of violence against women, and sports events from boxing to baseball feature scantily clad females for audience gawking.

Then there is the media stereotype of women which is fostered through situation comedies on TV and soft-porn magazines. Females are regarded as mindless bodies. They are for men to gape at and ogle, whistle at and tease, lust after and covet.

Some philosophers who are particularly concerned about language have begun to call attention to common terms of reference for women which carry an inherent disrespect. Instead of neutral terms like woman, lady, and girl, non-Christian males are typically given to referring to the opposite sex in gender-sexual terms, as playthings, or even as animals. So it has become: Who was that skirt/broad/ (part of the anatomy)? Say, that's some fox/filly/chick over there! Then, of course, there is lewd and suggestive talk that has a much more direct message. This sort of thing is not flattery to a self-respecting woman of intelligence and maturity. It is distasteful and abhorrent.

A woman walking the streets or functioning at her profession often has to confront what has come to be called "sexual harassment." It may be as subtle as a leer, as crude as a catcall or whistle, or as direct as a pinch. A typist in New York whose boss offered her a raise if she would sleep with him and a freshman at Harvard whose instructor tried to kiss her when she went to his office for a conference are among many women who have gone to court over this sort of treatment.

A secretary in Atlanta quit her job after her boss and three other men watched her lock a long row of filing cabinets and then called out, "Isn't she a cutie!" It is to be hoped that any Christian woman would feel insulted rather than flattered by such a quip. This lady summed it up by saying, "They strip you of your dignity."

The degree of a woman's purity can be indexed by little things. How do you react to "sexual harassment"? Do you blush and take offense at crude remarks, suggestive statements, and the like? Or do you dress and behave so as to call attention to your sexiness?

It distresses me that some of the most pointed challenges to sexist language and behavior in our culture come not from Christian ethicists but from radical feminists who speak from a humanistic point of view. For example, one has written:

> It is a fine, spring day, and with an utter lack of self-consciousness I am bouncing down the street. Suddenly I hear men's voices. Catcalls and whistles fill the air. These noises are clearly sexual in intent and they are meant for me; they come from a group of men hanging about a corner across the street. I freeze. As Sartre would say, I have been petrified by the gaze of the Other. My face flushes and my motions become stiff and self-conscious. The body which, only a moment before, I inhabited with such ease now floods my consciousness. I have been made into an object. ... There is an element of compulsion in this encounter, in this being-made-to-be-aware of one's own flesh; like being made to apologize, it is humiliating. It is unclear what role is played by sexual arousal or even sexual connoisseurship in encounters like these. The encounter described seems less the spontaneous expression of a healthy eroticism than a ritual of subjugation.[1]

Be very conscious of maintaining a chaste lifestyle, and be genuinely indignant when anyone tries to test, tease, or harass you. It demonstrates the sort of purity of heart that will tell a godly man that you are of real character. Do not consciously submit to the "rituals of subjugation" which have come to be common in our time.

In dating contexts, do not use your sexuality as bait for a man you think you love or allow yourself to jeopardize your self-respect by compromising your commitment to Christian chastity.

When you find that person whom you think you want to marry, don't jeopardize your relationship with him with "innocent flirtations" with other men. Be totally trustworthy in this matter of your purity.

Respectful

Third, a godly wife shows by her attitude and behavior the **respect for her husband** which she carries in her heart.

Depending on the translation of 1 Peter 3:2b which you are reading, the text refers to a wife's exhibition of "fear" (KJV, ASV), "reverence" (NIV), or being "reverent" (RSV). Most commentators take this to be a reference to her attitude of worshipful respect toward God.

It seems much more reasonable in context to interpret the respect of this passage as being directed toward her husband rather than God. If such is the case, the verse parallels Ephesians 5:33b: "the wife must respect (reverence, KJV; fear, ASV) her husband."

On this reading of the verse, Peter is talking about the way a woman relates to her husband in making him feel secure, building him up rather than tearing him down, not embarrassing him.

It is painful to watch some wives in relation to their husbands or, for that matter, some women in relation to men generally. They have felt victimized and stepped on by a man at some point in life and now feel compelled to get even. So little games of one-upsmanship are always being played. She likes to make her husband look small in front of other people or humiliate him before his friends. What this does to the relationship is not difficult to imagine.

As a single woman preparing for marriage, realize that not all men are alike. The fact that one might hurt or take advantage of you need not make you defensive toward all men. The fact that the person you dated and were in love with jilted you does not mean that you are entitled to string on some fellow who is doting on you. If you have been hurt by someone, put it behind you and try again to find someone you can love and trust. Don't make it a one-woman crusade to get even with all males of the species by showing them up as dumb, unfeeling creatures.

In a going-steady arrangement or after you are engaged, take occasional readings of your own maturity by the way you treat that man. When he needs encouragement and lifting of his confidence, are you the one who gives it to him? When he needs a bit of the air let out of his sails, can you find a way to do it without humiliating him?

Beautiful

Fourth, the apostle raises the issue of a woman's **beauty.**

The beauty of Sarah, wife of Abraham, has given rise to a number of legendary accounts in post-biblical Jewish literature. In Scripture itself, she is represented as being so beautiful at age 65 that Abraham feared he might be killed for her sake when they went into Egypt (Gen. 12:10-13; cf. 20). Peter praised her, however, for cultivating "the unfading beauty of a gentle and quiet spirit, which is of great worth in God's sight" (NIV).

Peter does not tell a woman to choose between outer and inner beauty. His statements about hair, jewelry, and clothing for the body on the one hand and inner beauty on the other should not be read as mutually exclusive possibilities. They should be interpreted in this way: *not only* should she pay attention to her physical charm *but also* to the grace and loveliness of her spirit – with emphasis on the latter.

It isn't too difficult to follow his meaning here. Most of us have been acquainted with the physically stunning woman whose conceit, self-centeredness, and petulance made being around her an unpleasant experience. Most of us have also had occasion to meet women who were not glamorous by the most generous of standards but whose grace, charm, and pleasant dispositions made them delightful company. A woman of the latter sort can be pardoned a pug nose or imperfect teeth; there is a deeper beauty that makes up for the deficiency. But there is nothing which can offset the flawed character of the other woman; her physical beauty is discounted and allowed to count for very little when seen in the light of her poverty of spirit.

Too many young women place heavy emphasis on their sexuality during dating years. Make-up, clothing, and carriage are chosen to emphasize certain features and body parts. Then they are upset when the guys they draw to themselves only want their bodies. If that is what you're advertising, that is what the opposite sex will want from you.

The sort of man you want to pay attention to you will be more impressed by genuine femininity than statuesque proportions and model-type features. Kindness, dignity, gentleness, thoughtfulness, and compassion are traits which reveal an inner beauty which will attract the sort of man whose attention you would be happy with for a lifetime.

What To Look For In A Man

Suppose, then, that you concentrate on Peter's counsel about what you should be. You cultivate an unselfish, Christian spirit in dealing with others. You keep your heart and life pure from moral defilement. You have a healthy and respectful attitude toward the opposite sex in general. And you nurture a feminine disposition which gives you the serene beauty of a confident but not brassy woman.

What type man do you look for now? In the next chapter, three qualities of crucial importance in the life of a Christian man will be discussed from the same biblical setting we have been examining in this chapter. They will help answer that question. For the time being, however, there is this general answer which suggests itself: *look for someone who appreciates and complements the character you have developed.*

First, look for someone whose life goals you respect and whose leadership you could follow. You will not find it easy to be submissive to a man whose career goals don't seem worthwhile to you or who is an indecisive wimp about everything.

Second, look for a man who is morally upright himself and who respects you for your purity. A man whose values are shaky and who presses you to compromise your own is not the one you need.

Third, look for a man you admire for himself. You want to marry someone whom you can respect for his character, integrity, and sense of loyalty to what is right – even if he doesn't achieve every good thing he dreams about or hit the career heights you envision for him.

Fourth, look for a man who appreciates your total beauty as a woman and treats you accordingly. If he cannot see beauty except at a skindeep level and has his head turned by every pretty face he sees, he evidently is not mature enough to appreciate the deeper feminine beauty which is worth so much more.

Conclusion

See yourself as the person of dignity, worth, and importance God made you. Respect yourself for who and what you are, for your special abilities, and for your spiritual potential.

Whether you are a high school or college woman, single or married, career woman or homemaker, let your life count for God's glory in this wicked world. Challenge the stereotypes and barriers our society has built around you in the strength of Jesus Christ.

4/ A Man Prepares
for Marriage

Where does one go in the Word of God to find the most
direct and practical counsel for a man who is thinking
about marriage?

Let's stay in the same chapter of the Bible we studied
in Chapter Three of this volume when we looked for scriptural insights into a woman's preparation for getting married. After six verses of instructions to women about the
fundamental traits of character which produce godly wives,
Peter uses a short, one-verse paragraph to identify three
principles which must be observed by men who want to
become good husbands.

Just at this point, someone may be wondering why Peter
used six verses to counsel women and only one to speak
to the men. (One lady even suggested that it would be
good to remember that this was written by *Mr.* Peter and
that *Mrs.* Peter might have reversed the ratio!) There is a
perfectly good reason for it.

When Peter wrote this epistle, he faced the harsh real-
ities of the cultural situation which existed. Society was
dominated by men who often treated women harshly. One
of the orthodox prayers used in the synagogue and in
private devotions by Jewish men goes this way: "Lord, I
thank you that you did not make me a Gentile, a slave, or
a woman." And Cato reflected the attitude of the larger

37

Roman world toward women when he wrote: "If you were to catch your wife in an act of infidelity, you can kill her with impunity without a trial; but, if she were to catch you, she would not venture to touch you with her finger, and, indeed, she has no right."

In a society where women were afforded few rights, more extensive instruction was given them for the sake of helping them deal with their situation – especially that of Christian women married to unbelieving men. Then Peter gave the following instruction to Christian men which would serve to elevate women in their eyes and make possible a healthy relationship between husbands and wives in Christian homes.

> Likewise you husbands, live considerately with your wives, bestowing honor on the woman as the weaker sex, since you are joint heirs of the grace of life, in order that your prayers may not be hindered (1 Pet. 3:7 RSV).

As in the previous chapter, our concern with *preparation* for marriage will take us to this verse to find the personality traits which a man can work to develop before his wedding day.

Understanding

First, Christian husbands need to be *understanding* men who know how to treat women with consideration and sensitivity.

Archie Bunker's condescending attitude toward women is well known to people who remember the old "All in the Family" television series. He was the stereotypical male who constantly showed contempt for his wife, Edith. "Stifle yourself, Edith!" was his classic line to shut her up when she had an opinion to express or an independent idea.

In explaining to his neighbor, Irene, how he could treat his wife that way, Archie once laid out his general theory of the relationship between the sexes. In the TV episode in question, he was explaining why women should be paid less for doing the same job as men. "C'mon, Irene," says Archie, "its a well-known fact that men are worth more than women. In the Bible it says God made man in his own image and then made woman from a rib – a cheaper cut." The line was good for a laugh. The pity of it is that some men seem to take this "macho image" of disrespect for women seriously.

Disrespect for and frustration of women is not the biblical way. There is no way to justify the hard, cold, and indifferent attitude of some husbands toward their wives. Surely it comes about in a marriage because a pattern for disrespect for females has been cultivated – perhaps even unconsciously – in the background of those men.

In order for a husband to be understanding of his wife, he must have the ability to listen to her point of view. He must listen not only to her words but to her feelings. He must know how to be selfless in order to get into her ideas and needs. Then he can try to meet those needs in caring ways.

People who work as professional marriage counselors speak and write constantly about communication in marriage. The Bible has always pointed to the crucial nature of communication.

To his contemporaries, Jesus said this prophecy from Isaiah was being fulfilled among them: "You will be ever hearing but never understanding; you will be ever seeing but never perceiving" (Matt. 13:14). Are husbands sometimes guilty of the same sort of spiritual deafness and blindness toward their wives as those people were toward Jesus? Do men sometimes fail to see what they are doing to their wives through their neglect and lack of understanding?

Some husbands come home from work and immediately bury themselves in things which isolate them from their wives and/or children. There may be no sinister intent involved. He may just be doing the yard work or watching television. There is nothing wrong with those things – unless they are being allowed to prevent or disrupt needed communication. His wife may have been at home with the baby all day and in desperate need of adult conversation, but she gets the busy signal when trying to get his attention. If this keeps up, she can become lonely and unhappy in their marriage.

Just listening to another person says at least this much: I am interested in you and what is going on in your world.

James Dobson is one of the most widely read and respected authors of our time. He has written a helpful little book entitled *What Wives Wish Their Husbands Knew About Women.*[1] Although written for people who are already married, it would be a useful thing for a man about to get married to read the book for its insights into female personality. It would help prevent a number of misunderstandings from developing into monumental problems in a husband-wife relationship. The book's pervasive theme of building a woman's self-esteem through a healthy marriage relationship is important.

A man who is contemplating marriage needs to look at himself closely for signs of understanding and sensitivity to women generally and to his fiancee in particular. If you can't bring yourself to listen to a woman, respect her point of view on a matter, and be considerate of her feelings about things, you likely cannot pass Peter's first test for a good husband.

Protective

Second, Christian husbands are men who "treat [their wives] with respect as the weaker sex" (NIV) and assume the *protector role* within the marriage.

Women are generally "weaker" than men in only one way – physical strength. Because they are not as rugged as men, Christian men feel a special sense of responsibility to look out for their welfare. This is particularly true of Christian husbands in relation to their wives.

You may have travelled in the East and seen men riding on animals while their wives walked along in the heat and dust. In many cultures it is considered improper for men to defer to women. They prove themselves to be strong by ignoring or victimizing women. Vestiges of this same wrong-

40

headed notion of male-to-female relationships survive in our own culture.

There is even a romanticized image of violence against women which glorifies it. Do you remember the scene in *Gone With the Wind* where Rhett swings Scarlett off her feet, crushes her body against his own, and takes her struggling and screaming up the stairs? Literature and cinema are filled with scenes of domestic force which perpetuate the myth of its acceptability. Men have the right to control and chastise the women in their lives; women have the duty to submit –if not a longing to enjoy it.

Some women may have a masochistic streak, but surely they are the rare, sick exceptions to the rule.

Violence against women in our society is horrifying in its frequency and brutality.[2] Rapes, including gang rapes and rapes of children, are reported on practically every newscast. Yet, according to an aggregate of surveys done by the U.S. Census Bureau, the FBI, and the National Opinion Research Center, only 3.5 percent to 10 percent of rapes are reported in this country. A woman's chance of being raped at some point in her life is an appalling one in 10.

Police, hospitals, and courts are treating rape victims more intelligently of late, conviction rates are going up, and judges are more likely than they once were to give stiff sentences to offenders. We are beginning to understand that rape is not an act of sexual passion but of aggression, power, and anger against women. The director of a sex-offender program at the state prison in Somers, Connecticut, says of rapists: "They are insecure, inadequate people who don't feel in control of their own lives or themselves." So they rape women to establish their control over someone else, their power. There is sometimes violence against women within their marriages. Marital abuse is what some people refer to as the "silent crime." Legal structures and social service networks across the United States, prompted by grass-roots appeals from women, have begun to see wife beating and other forms of violence against women as violations of the victim's civil rights and as criminal acts of assault.

Christian men are aware of the vulnerability of women and are willing to assume the responsibility for assisting them in protecting themselves. They treat women with respect and consideration; they protect them from dangerous or potentially hurtful situations. Even in the little things, the practice of old-fashioned chivalry toward the females in their lives has not died. They open umbrellas and pull cars to the door. They carry bundles and open doors. They don't feel compelled to show off as "tough guys" by pushing around, hitting, or otherwise intimidating women. They are secure enough in their own self-image that they do not see themselves as "wimps" for behaving in a caring and polite manner.

A man who shows gentlemanly solicitude for a woman's well-being during courtship likely will be considerate of her after the wedding. He won't let his wife overwork herself. He will know when to take her away for a break or week-end without the responsibility of the children. And he won't let his children treat their mother with disrespect. He is her protector.

Jesus died to protect his bride from harm. His perfect love for the church is every man's model of how he should love and protect his wife (cf. Eph. 5:21-33).

Treat As Spiritual Equal

Third, husbands are to acknowledge their wives "as *heirs with you of the gracious gift of life*, so that nothing will hinder your prayers" (NIV).

Women do not depend on men for their spiritual status before God. Their salvation does not come through their fathers or husbands; it comes through their personal relationship with Jesus Christ. In Christ there is no distinction of access into divine grace for men and women. Male and female are "one in Christ Jesus" and "heirs according to promise" as the spiritual descendants of Abraham (Gal. 3:26-29). They will share equally in the future inheritance which is reserved for the children of God.

This means that a woman is directly responsible to God

in the matter of her salvation and spiritual maturity. Her assigned role is not always the same as that of the man in church organization, yet her dignity, worth, and responsibility are no less significant than his before God.

In fact, Peter makes it clear that a man jeopardizes his own spiritual status before the Lord by failing to acknowledge his wife as his spiritual equal. What else can he mean by the warning against having one's prayers "hindered"? A man who is inconsiderate of his wife, fails to act as her protector, or denigrates her spiritual life jeopardizes his own relationship with heaven.

The role of a man in relation to a woman in spiritual things should be one of affirming rather than denying, of supporting rather than discouraging. He should lead her to greater involvement with service to Christ and the church. Some of this involvement will come in the form of joint activity. Some of it will involve personal ministry by her alone or in connection with other women. Instead of resenting the fact that these things make demands on his wife, he should be pleased that she feels a sense of spiritual drive to participate in them and do what he can to make it possible for her to do so.

In their private devotional life, they should share in the joys of Bible study and prayer.

In the maintenance of their home, she should feel as free as he does to use the things at their disposal to meet needs, show hospitality, and share the gospel.

Scripture makes the point again and again that people cannot be right with God if they are creating wrong relationships with one another (cf. 1 John 4:20). We sometimes forget that this principle applies to male-female relationships in courtship and marriage. Peter calls it to our attention in a direct and forceful way. A man interrupts his relationship with God when he denies respect and right treatment to his wife.

Some women live with a real spiritual burden because of their husbands. They are only marginally involved with the church and do not have the liberty to use their homes for personal ministry.

As a man prepares for marriage, then, he must acknowledge the truth that God loves women just as much as men. Let him admire a woman not only for her beauty, social grace, and intelligence but for her spirituality as well. Let the two of them build a relationship with one another which has Christ at the center and which is heavy on involvement with the things of the kingdom of God.

What To Look For In A Woman

What does such a man look for in a woman?

Going back to the first six verses of 1 Peter 3, he should look for a woman who shows an unselfish disposition, is chaste in her behavior, shows respect for you, and concentrates on the inner beauty of Christian character.

Then, in light of the qualities of a Christian husband which have been identified in verse 7 and discussed in this chapter, *look for a woman who has a personality consistent with the demands God has made of you in relation to the woman you will marry.*

First, look for someone who will allow you to understand her. That is, find a woman who will be honest with you, think with you, and give you a chance to know her needs and desires. Communication is a two-way street and cannot take place between two people when either of them is so defensive that he or she cannot open his or her heart to the other.

Second, look for a woman who trusts you. God has made you the protector of your wife. Thus you will need to marry a woman who regards you as competent to look out for her welfare. If she makes it clear that she intends to be independent of you (i.e., financially, socially, etc.), you are being told that you will never be allowed to fill the role God has given you as her protector.

Third, look for a woman who is truly interested in spiritual things. A woman who prefers movies or concerts to worship, who has no concern for Bible reading and prayer as part of your relationship, or who has a heart which is oriented to things which will take both of you away from God is not the person with whom you need to join your life –and destiny.

Conclusion

The Bible makes it clear that Christian marriage involves what might be called *double submission.* "Subject yourselves one to another in the fear of Christ," says Paul to husbands and wives (Eph. 5:21).

Because the man and woman involved see each other's reverence for Christ, they know they can trust each other fully. A man's love for God gives his wife the confidence to submit to him; a woman's love for God makes her husband willing to turn his life over to her. Each submits to the other out of their mutual understanding of Christ's will for their life together.

This ideal pattern for double submission must be kept in mind in selecting a mate, for you want to marry someone whom you love and respect as is rather than someone you think you can change. You want to marry someone who brings out the best in you. You want to marry a Christian.

5/ Virtues for All Seasons

Just as there are seasons in the year, there are seasons to life. To quote from an old yet still familiar song: "It's a long, long while from May to December/ And the days grow short when you reach September." There are seasons in marriage, too.

Each season of the year has its special delights. The crisp, clear mornings of winter, the greening time of spring, the pleasant summer evenings, the beautiful colors of autumn – each season of the year is unique to itself. One dresses differently, eats differently, and plans life differently in the various seasons.

Each season of a marriage has its special features. The thrill of early love, the delight in the arrival of a child, the growth experiences with one another and your children, adjustments to the children's departure from home, retirement years – each is unique and holds its special challenges. You must be aware of the changing seasons of a marriage and plan, think, and live appropriately to each one.

Over the next few chapters, we will examine some of the "seasons" you can expect in your married life. From how to begin the adventure through the joys and problems of being parents to the climactic years of life shared with your mate, we will look at some of the more predictable things to expect and talk about some productive methods of dealing with them positively.

In this chapter, however, I want to identify a trio of qualities which need to be constant through all the periods of married life: *love, faithfulness, and forgiveness.*

Love

The primary constant in a successful home environment is love.

Christian love (Gk, *agape*) is not fickle affection, candles and soft music, or something two people can "make" by bringing each other to heights of sexual ecstasy. It is one person's willingness to seek another's happiness or well-being at the sacrifice, if need be, of one's own interests.

I am acutely aware that the giving of a definition for the term "love" seems rather bland. The word has subjective connotations to each of us that cannot be captured in a formal statement. While not denying these subjective features, they are not of its essence. In fact, self-giving concern for another person need not have positive emotional feelings attached to it. How else can we understand Jesus' command to love our enemies? (Matt. 5:44). We cannot feel tender affection for people who have done us evil; we can, however, return good for evil and thus conquer evil with love (cf. Rom. 12:20-21).

> *Agape* love is plugged into an eternal power source, and it can go on operating when every other kind of love fails. Not only that! It loves, no matter what. No matter how unlovable the other person is, *agape* can keep on flowing. *Agape* is as unconditional as God's love for us. It is a mental attitude based on a deliberate choice of the will ...[1]

Within marriage, love certainly should be (and most often is) associated with feelings of attachment, desire, and warmth. But we must understand that love itself is not a capricious emotion which comes and goes unpredictably and uncontrollably. Love is a deliberate, purposeful, and directed action. It is not the excitement of an unstable emotion but the governed act of one's intellect and will. Only when understood this way can we believe it is possible to maintain love at every season of a marriage.

Because Christians have been loved of God (i.e., he sought our good when we were not lovable or cooperative), we should know more than others can about how to love one another. "Dear friends, let us love one another, for love comes from God. Everyone who loves has been born of God and knows God. Whoever does not love does not know God, because God is love. ... Dear friends, since God so loved us, we also ought to love one another" (1 John 4:7-8a,11).

The passage just cited from 1 John has reference to the love which members of the family of God, the church, ought to have for one another. Surely what is said here ought to apply with particular force to the most intimate love relationship two humans can share with one another. A Christian man and woman ought to be able to create a marriage climate which abounds in love at all seasons.

From reading 1 Corinthians 13, one gets a good practical description of the difference love makes in a marriage. The partners are patient and kind with one another and any children God may give them. One does not envy the other's abilities or boast of his or her successes in such a way as to "put down" the other person. Neither gives pride the upper hand.

Rudeness and self-seeking are out of place in a Christian home. Tempers are kept under control by divine aid, and nobody in the house dwells on others' faults or keeps a running total of the wrongs suffered at their hands. They look for ways to protect rather than injure, believe the best about each other, and stand together to face life's disappointments.

Heaven wants husbands to love their wives as much as they love themselves. "In the same way, husbands ought to love their wives as their own bodies. ... However, each one of you also must love his wife as he loves himself" (Eph. 5:28a, 33a). He wants them to love their wives at all seasons of their relationship as Christ has loved his church. "Husbands, love your wives, just as Christ also loved the church and gave himself up for her" (Eph. 5:25). And he wants wives to love their husbands as totally and unreservedly as he wants their husbands to love them.

In Paul's frightening description of people who "did not think it worthwhile to retain the knowledge of God," he said one of their traits was "heartless" behavior or a lack of "natural affection" (Rom. 1:31, cf. ASV). The word in the original text refers to people who lack the normal feelings of positive concern for their own flesh and blood which would prompt the display of love within a family circle.

Paul likely intended for his readers to understand the term to refer to those who abuse their family members. Wife beating and child abuse were common sins in the first-century world. They have not disappeared yet!

According to a cover story in *Time* magazine which was cited in Chapter Four of this book, approximately six million wives will suffer physical abuse in any given calendar year; battery is the single major cause of injury to women, more significant than car accidents, rapes, or mugging; some 2,000 to 4,000 women are beaten to death annually; the nation's police departments spend one-third of their time responding to domestic-violence calls.

Child abuse cases are getting headlines across the nation. In 1976 polls showed that only about ten percent of Americans considered violence against children a serious national problem; a Louis Harris poll in 1983 revealed that 90 percent of Americans now see it as a problem. The National Center on Child Abuse and Neglect says that between 60,000 and 100,000 children are sexually abused by their own parents every year, and approximately 5,000 die from abuse inflicted by their parents.

Sins against one's own family members are signs of alienation from God. Where God's presence is found in a home through loving commitment, people cannot treat each other with disrespect. A man and woman are one flesh, and to hurt that partner would be to wound one's own self; children in their home are precious trusts from God and can be loved most when they deserve it least – just as God has loved us.

At all seasons and in all relationships within their unit, people living together in a Christian home love each other, build up each other, and minister to each other's needs.

Faithfulness

A second virtue for all seasons of marriage is faithfulness.

Faith in God is one's willingness to trust in and submit to him on the basis of his integrity. It is taking him at his word and knowing that his word will not fail. "Now faith is being sure of what we hope for and certain of what we do not see" (Heb. 11:1).

Faith is closely related to faithfulness. Our trust in God and willingness to obey him are in direct proportion to our confidence in his faithfulness. Only if we are certain that he will do what he has promised can we submit to him in joy. It is my personal conviction that one's ability to believe in God is directly related to the experience he or she has within a family unit. Let me illustrate and draw from this idea.

Think first of the situation with the children who will enter the home at a certain season of a marriage. Since we think of God as "Father" and are taught in Scripture to see ourselves as "children of God," surely the experiences we have with our own fathers in the flesh will color the way we can conceive of God the Father.

Suppose you are a child living in a family unit where the husband and father is a godly man who loves his family and is totally faithful to them. He cares about his wife and involves himself directly in the lives of his children. He is honest, fair, and able to give wise counsel. As his child, you love him with your whole heart and think of him as the best father in the world. In such a context, what would be the significance of having God presented to you under the figure of fatherhood?

Now suppose you are a child living in a home where the husband and father is a covenant breaker. He is unfaithful to his wife and often stays away from home at night. When he is at home, he seems to make it his preoccupation to throw the house into turmoil. You are occasionally frightened when he is around and actually prefer those nights at home when he does not show up. In this context, what do you think your response would be to the notion of the fatherhood of God? Might you have problems?

If the children in a given family are unable to put their complete confidence in their parents – particularly their father – then it is going to be hard for them to be attracted to the biblical portrait of God the Father. In order to appreciate it, they will have to overthrow the image of fatherhood they have known best. It is not impossible, but it is terribly difficult and can be achieved only with conscious effort. How much better it is to be able to transfer a positive attitude toward one's father in the flesh to the Father in heaven.

I was so fortunate in this regard. My own father was my ideal of Christian manhood. His word was "good as gold," and every action of his toward me – even in situations where I had disappointed him or proved myself unworthy of his kindness – was a loving action. He made it easy for me to have faith in my Heavenly Father.

The same principle also works between the two adult partners to a marriage. Time and again, I have seen it happen that people would lose interest in and withdraw from the church because of problems they were having in their marriages. At first it seemed very strange. After all, wasn't this the time above all others that an individual would need God and the support of his or her spiritual family? But there is just something so devastating about "breaking faith" between two people that leaves even the faithful party feeling defeated, empty, and wondering whether there is any use in going on. Not a few persons in such a circumstance think seriously about suicide – and some carry through on the thought.

It is such a common phenomenon in our society that we have coined a term to describe it: *mid-life crazy.* Some men appear to need the reassurance of their desirability from women other than their wives. Perhaps frustrated by failures or unrealized dreams at this point in life when their most productive years appear to be behind them, they need to prove themselves by altering grooming habits, spending money foolishly, altering their personalities, and/or having an affair. Syndicated columnist Bob Greene published the following letter which had been written to him:

I am a 51-year-old woman. Right now I am suffering from the devastation of being fired. For over 30 years I devoted my life to the job I had. Now I'm not very young anymore, and my prospects are very slim of being rehired or of finding another job. ... You see, I have just been relieved of my duties as a wife.

My very successful husband has informed me that he no longer requires my services. He is looking for someone with less practical experience and more advanced techniques ... techniques gleaned from the pages of the *Playboy, Penthouse,* and *Hustler* magazines that are strewn around in his fancy new apartment. Plenty of applicants seek my former job. His new look of trimness and tan, plenty of money, and no family responsibilities make his job opening the most sought-after position in town. He even gives flowers, trips, and gifts to any and all who show interest – fringe benefits he felt unnecessary for his former employee....

I was always so proud to bear my husband's name. Now another woman will be assuming the same name ... one I upheld for years and zealously guarded from even the slightest taint of tarnish. I doubt she'll be as careful. Many times I've held the pillow over my face to keep neighbors from hearing the screams in the night.[2]

I have no way of knowing whether this lady's letter affects you as it did me when I first read it. Perhaps it tugged at my heart because a friend had been given her "notice of termination" about two weeks before it was published in our local paper. Here was my response to both situations: How can these women ever trust anybody again? Having been betrayed and tossed aside by their husbands, would they henceforth be so cynical as to distrust the word of everybody? Might they even lose faith in God and his Word?

My wife and I were recently talking in our den with a

woman whose husband had lately left her, revealed a long-standing affair with another woman, and begun living with his new lover. She was struggling with some confused feelings which just couldn't be put into words with "the preacher and his wife." So I shared the letter above with her and shared my theory of how such an experience could conceivably turn a person on God and undermine Christian faith. She blurted out, "That's exactly how I feel. I haven't wanted to go to church. I can't pray. I've been afraid I was going to lose my faith!"

You may reply by saying that such a response would be unjustified and irrational. You are right, of course. But the fact remains that many people do react to such events in their lives by renouncing God. A woman (or man) is betrayed by the man she loves more than life itself. She is so consumed with grief that she simply loses the *ability* to believe. Her power to trust another human being has been trampled on and abolished; her ability to trust God may go at the same time. It may be irrational, but it happens nonetheless. Objectivity gets lost in the painful experience of having one's heart broken by an act of betrayal.

We must have homes where faith can exist without betrayal. Husbands and wives must be honest with one another. They must never break faith with one another. They must be totally trustworthy before their children. Otherwise the ability of the people in that family to believe in either God or one another may be impaired forever.

At every season of the marriage, let these words from the Lord God ring in your ears: "So guard yourself in your spirit, and do not break faith" (Mal. 2:16b).

Forgiveness

A third quality needed to make a marriage work at all seasons is forgiveness.

Because of the intimate nature of marriage, it is inevitable that a husband will sometimes offend his wife and vice versa. Because we are human, we are going to do thoughtless things at times which will hurt our partners. In the growth years of children and while their parents are making so many decisions affecting them, mistakes will be made by immature children and imperfect mothers and fathers. Even in the best of homes, there will be times which call for penitence and free forgiveness among its members.

God is eager to pardon us when we sin against him. "You are forgiving and good, O Lord, abounding in love to all who call to you" (Psa. 86:5). No penitent person need ever fear to seek divine forgiveness, for there is no reluctance on God's part to be gracious with his pardon. This divine model should be imitated by us humans when we sin against one another. Thus we are taught: "Be kind and compassionate to one another, forgiving each other, just as in Christ God forgave you" (Eph. 4:32).

Several years ago, I worked for quite a long time in an unsuccessful effort to keep two people from divorce. The pair involved were bright and made a fine-looking couple. They had a great deal going for them. But the man's inability to forgive his wife of a sin she committed before they were married destroyed their relationship.

She had committed fornication with a man she had dated before meeting the man who would become her husband. After she had married, her husband began to press her for the details of her life before they had met. Then he specifically wanted to know about her relationship with the man she had dated just prior to meeting him. And he forced her to relate every sordid detail of their sin. As she told him of what had happened, she tearfully pleaded for his forgiveness and repeatedly assured him that she loved him too much to be guilty of ever betraying him in the future.

He could not handle what he had insisted on knowing about his wife. He wrote out a "confession" of sorts and had her to sign it. He proceeded to carry that paper in his wallet. On occasion, he would pull it out and have his wife read it aloud to him – through her blinding tears. He simply would not forgive her!

People about to get married sometimes ask my advice about telling the prospective mate of some past sin. Here is the counsel I offer them: If the sin you have committed is widely known or otherwise likely to be learned about someday by the person you are preparing to marry, tell him or her of it, explain that you have repented and been forgiven of it, and ask his or her forgiveness. Otherwise, keep it to yourself.

Here is the reasoning behind such a view: If it is not necessary for that person to know of your past sin for the sake of his or her own protection against being hurt somewhere down the line, telling of the event will only serve to put an unnecessary burden on the person who must bear it. So, unless telling of some past sin is necessary to set the matter right or to help assure good relationships in the future, repent of it and leave the matter with God.

Someone may ask, "But doesn't the Bible tell us to confess our sins to one another?" Yes, it does. But the requirement of James 5:16 has been tragically misused of late. It has been used by some to promote the baring of one's innermost secrets and most private thoughts. James 5:16 is encouraging one who has committed a sin already known to others to confess that sin so they (1) will know of his penitence and (2) be able to pray for his forgiveness in an intelligent manner. This verse has nothing to do with the "secret sins" of one's past. It is an unhealthy thing to go prying into others' closets in search of skeletons.

During the season of marriage which involves the presence of children, there will be times requiring patience, forgiveness, and healing. Children sometimes get in trouble at school or with the law. They can get involved with alcohol, drugs, or sex. A daughter can become pregnant. Without minimizing the sin or excusing the wrong that has been done, parents need to be the most supportive figures in the lives of those children in helping them set things straight.

I think, for example, of two men in different cities who had sons who got involved with drugs at age 17. One father raved and ranted, locked his son out of his house, and let everyone know he no longer claimed the boy as his own. The other father prayed in his grief for God's wisdom, sat with his son during a trial to give him constant assurance of his love, and spent fully a year of his life in working with that boy to bring him out of his problem. The former boy wound up in the penitentiary; the latter is now a college graduate, married, and active in helping troubled young people through his congregation's youth program.

Most of the situations which will call for the exercise of forgiveness within a family unit will not be of great magnitude. They will involve the need to forgive trivial offenses and petty wrongs. Strange as it may seem, however, most people seem to find it harder to admit guilt or extend pardon in trivial matters than in great ones. Some people who could forgive adultery or drug use seem not to be able to tolerate a partner who squeezes the toothpaste tube in the middle or a child who likes loud music. The countless little things are what make or break a family.

If you find it hard to apologize when you have been wrong, you need to pray about that fault daily until you overcome it. If you tend to justify yourself or parade another's faults instead of accepting responsibility for a wrong you have done, you need to rein in your ego before you destroy your home. If you tend to pout and hold grudges, you need to remember these words from Jesus: "But if ye forgive not men their trespasses, neither will your Father forgive your trespasses" (Matt. 6:15).

Conclusion

Love, faithfulness, and forgiveness will serve your family well in all seasons. In fact, you dare not try to negotiate any period of your life without them.

Now let's look at some of the particular seasons of married life and some of the specific things which can be done to make each a positive and spiritual experience of love.

6/ Beginning the Adventure

How important is a good beginning to a marriage? Particularly, how crucial is the first year of marriage?

That the early days of a couple's life together are more important than even they may realize is indicated by a piece of Old Testament legislation. In a culture where it was urgent that every man have descendants to perpetuate his name, God ordered the commanders of the army to exempt certain individuals from military service. Beyond the cultural circumstance, the text indicates a further practical purpose to be served by such an exemption. "If a man has recently married, he must not be sent to war or have any other duty laid on him. For one year he is free to stay at home and bring happiness to the wife he has married" (Deut. 24:5; cf. 20:5-9). Quite an extended honeymoon, eh?

Our modern custom of a honeymoon may trace to this ancient practice of the Israelites. No one is really sure of its origin, and this is much more likely than some which have been suggested. A further vestige of this piece of legislation is seen in the fact that until recently marriage was a ground for deferring one's call-up to military service in the United States.

That first year really is significant to a marriage. Initial adjustments will be made which determine the nature of the pair's relationship henceforth. In those first accommodations to each other, a pattern of tolerance and cooperation or resistance and friction is established which will either make or break the relationship.

It is a widely known and frequently discussed fact: marriages that fail tend to do so in the first year. So the first year of marriage really is a critical time. It is the foundation-laying year for the entire relationship. Build on a solid foundation, and the house stands; build on the sand, and a collapse will come somewhere down the line.

Patterns of Adjustment

Adjustments have to be made at various stages of a marriage. There are some rather predictable times which all couples should expect and prepare to handle.

First, there is the period of initial adjustment to each other at the time of marriage. Second, all those initial accommodations have to be refined as children come into the family. Third, about the time a couple has worked out its life in relation to their children, the children leave home and create new adjustment problems. Fourth, retirement and the major changes which accompany aging require still more adjustment. Fifth, there will be crisis situations faced at all stages of the marriage; job loss, serious illness/injury, and eventually the death of one partner are just a few examples.

Not only are the cycles of adjustment predictable; so are the patterns.

The most destructive adjustment pattern is marked by constant friction over issues. The two people quarrel openly about some issue and never come to a satisfactory solution. Each digs the other. One or both may bring it up in public settings and try to embarrass the other person. Sharp words are exchanged, and behavior such as pouting or sleeping on the couch emphasizes the impasse.

John may be accustomed to playing golf on Saturdays or going bowling with the guys on Thursday evenings;

Marsha may want him to spend that time with her rather than his old friends. They may have a tug-of-war over it. He serves notice that he "won't be bossed around" by his wife and told what he can or can't do with his free time; she accuses him of caring more about his friends than his wife and being insensitive to her needs for his time. The same fight is had over and over again – every week without fail.

This marriage will self-destruct before very long.

A better way of handling adjustment involves mutual accommodation in the face of a challenge. The bitterness and open hostility are replaced by quiet acceptance. Neither is particularly pleased with the state of affairs, and the topic sometimes comes up for discussion. There is something important enough to them, however, that they try to keep the matter on a back burner and avoid conflict. Their religious conviction that the marriage must stay together or a desire to present a united front to the children may provide the motivation to endure an irritation.

John still plays golf or goes bowling; Marsha wishes he were at home instead of out with the guys. But she accepts it without making a fuss every time he leaves the house. She may do something herself with that time to distract her from his absence. She has decided, however, that it would be foolish to hide his clubs or bowling ball, stand in front of the door and scream at him, or ruin every day of the week over a once-a-week situation she dislikes.

This marriage may endure without apparent conflict.

The best way to deal with differences is by finding a middle ground of compromise which makes both parties happy. Each cares enough about the other to look for a way to handle the adjustment without either having to lose face or suffer defeat.

John and Marsha may play golf or bowl together. They may find other couples to go to the links with them, or they may join a mixed league. If Marsha doesn't like either golf or bowling, John and she may take up tennis. The two of them are committed to using all aspects of their life together to solidify their relationship. Nothing is going to be allowed to remain a divisive issue.

Dealing With Change

Both circumstances and people change. This means that adjustments will have to be made constantly over the course of a marriage relationship. When people are flexible and caring, their pattern of handling change can solidify their relationship.

The best marriages are mutually supportive and leave room for both individuals to grow. They keep communication lines open so that conflicts can be resolved and exhibit a strong sense of commitment.

There is trouble ahead if either person is so strong-willed and opinionated that new ideas are not even weighed, if one partner has a definition of the other's role in mind and cannot tolerate any deviation from that fixed idea, or if one wants to grow while the other wants to keep everything just as it always has been.

Change can be threatening. Yet it *can* be viewed as an exciting opportunity for growth. Handled together and with mutual support, it can contribute positively to a relationship.

The following is a list of the basic challenges which will face a couple in the first year of marriage. Handling each in a positive way is crucial.

The Early Tasks of Marriage

The first task of marriage is getting acquainted.

People who date for a long time and/or have an extended engagement do better with their first-year adjustments. The reason seems obvious. The time they have spent together has allowed them to learn each other's personality, tastes, and quirks. They already have an awareness of the differences as well as similarities between them. They have already begun working through their differences and have established a pattern for coping with change and unexpected crises.

If the couple has not had an extended courtship and engagement, they will have to test themselves not only with each other but with each other's families. They will have to learn each other's basic likes and dislikes in food, recreation, friends, social events, etc.

No matter the length of pre-marital acquaintance, there are some things which cannot be learned about the other person until after the wedding.

Now you are sharing living space. Who gets what space in the small closet and how many drawers in the dresser? How neat is he/she with the bathroom? Now you are with each other at all hours of the day. Is he/she grouchy first thing in the morning? Now you are sexual partners. What will his/her expectations be in your sex life? Now you are financial partners. Who will handle the books? Will the budget you have drawn up really work, or will you be strapped with money problems?

Second, there is the matter of defining roles as husband and wife.

Many stereotypes exist in our minds about what is "wifely" and what is "husbandly." Some of those will influence you even unconsciously. Thus a husband and wife may both be working, yet the husband may not help with housework because that doesn't fit with his image of the male role in a family. The wife is taken advantage of and may come to resent it. On the other hand, the woman may resent having to work. Her image of a wife may place her at home; her image of a husband may have him more successful and a better provider than her husband can be at this point.

It is important that both the man and woman see their relationship as a freeing-up relationship rather than a confinement. This means, among other things, that they work out their own understanding of what a husband-wife relationship is. Working within the parameters of the Bible's guidelines for a man and woman in marriage, the two of them experiment and discover what works to make their life pattern satisfactory.

The third area of adjustment requires establishing new relationships with other persons in the newly married couple's life.

Both sets of parents now have to be viewed differently than ever before. Following the counsel of the Bible, both bride and groom must "leave" their parental families and "cleave" to one another (Gen. 2:24). The ideal is to have a close and loving relationship with those families while being independent of them. Marriage marks the final stage of growth in the life of a man or woman in relation to his or her parents; the child-parent relationship is now replaced by an adult-adult relationship.

Then there are the friends and social acquaintances of the couple. A married man and woman have different relationships with people in their sphere of social contact than do single people. A single man may spend a good deal of his social energies trying to impress the opposite sex and sorting out his options in relation to certain females; a married man is supposed to focus his attention and energy on one woman. A single woman may indulge in innocent flirtations with a wide circle of men; a married woman must not. If the new couple is slow about making its transition from the perspective and behavior of single adults to conduct appropriate to married persons, major problems can arise quickly.

Fourth, the young married couple must assist each other in finding personal identity and feeling secure in that identity.

I know all the jokes about "finding myself." I am also aware that there is a narcissistic view of personal identity which stands over against a Christian's surrender of himself or herself to the authority of Jesus Christ. By speaking here of "personal identity," nothing sinister is intended.

The identity which every man and woman must establish has to do with their functional place within the world they inhabit.

A man's identity is largely wrapped up in his work or career. He identifies a dream and begins to pursue it in his twenties. Time is committed to education or special training. He faces the normal insecurities of beginning to function in his field and to deal with competition and setbacks. He may discover that he has made a wrong career choice and have to start over or redirect his energies.

A woman's identity may be much less individualistic than the man's. Even if she is pursuing a career, studies have been done which confirm the view that women tend to define their identities in terms of relationships rather than functions. In the past couple of decades, there have been variations on this theme. Some women establish themselves in a career and delay marriage until their thirties; other women still marry in their twenties, have children, and then make an entry into the career world.

It isn't hard to see how these searches for fulfillment and self-esteem can complicate a young marriage. Marsha marries John thinking that he is going to pursue a certain career; he decides that field isn't for him, and he goes another direction with his work. This puts her in the position of having to make several adjustments of her own. John is going back to school when she thought that was behind them. They have a new circle of friends. They may have to move to a new part of the country. The changes begin to be compounded in every area of their life.

Perhaps Marsha is still working in the early stages of the marriage. In her career field, she has to be assertive, competitive, and in control. Yet in her marriage relationship she needs to be warm, noncompetitive, and in subjection to her husband. Two different roles have to be maintained simultaneously. It is no small task to manage this sort of challenge. The strains can become enormous.

If two people are spiritual enough that they have found their primary identities in Christ, a bond exists between them which is strong enough to hold them together until education, job, social circles, and the other elements of personal self-esteem are worked out. In the absence of that bond, things can come flying apart.

A fifth task of early marriage requires a couple to be able to make room for a child.

Oh, I know. Most couples don't intend to have children in the first year of marriage. The plan calls for work, saving, maturing, and then children. But the arrival of babies is not always according to plan. In spite of the Pill and the best of intentions, young brides do get pregnant.

Any two people who decide to marry must be prepared to accept the responsibility of being parents. If they are not mature enough or responsible enough to handle parenthood, they would be well advised to postpone their marriage.

The arrival of a child should draw the two adults closer together and provide still another dimension to their love. A study presented at the 1984 meeting of the American Sociological Association supports the view that having a baby does stabilize a marriage. A study of 5,284 non-parents and 5,540 new parents was conducted by the Rand Corporation. Ranging in age from 25 to 35, these young adults were followed for three years. The study showed that by the time their children were two years old, the parents had a divorce rate under eight percent; the non-parents had a divorce rate of more than 20 percent. One of the Rand sociologists said, "What people ignore ... is that after you become a parent you have a bond with your partner through your child." Having a baby to save a marriage is a foolish program, but babies do tend to strengthen the homes they enter.

Children shouldn't have to come into the world unwanted and resented. Couples shouldn't have their relationship strained over the arrival of children. Whether two people are prepared for the responsibility and able to accept a child with joy is something to be thought through carefully before the wedding ceremony.

Conclusion

A Christian marriage is one in which both husband and wife are consciously submitted to the will of God. It is a home where the partners are surrendered to the way of life described in the Word of God.

The first year of a marriage will generally chart its course. It is important to get started right.

7/ The Power of
a Listening Ear

The theme of this chapter is *communication in marriage.*

Every preacher, counselor, or friend of a person whose marriage was in trouble has heard the lament: "If we could only talk about things. We shout and accuse, but we don't really talk. We just don't communicate."

When the problem is traced back, the sad fact usually emerges that their isolation in silence began shortly after the wedding. There seems to be a pattern here. We pursue one another through letters, telephone calls, and long conversations. Every topic is important, and we hang on each other's words. Then there is a wedding ceremony and the felt need of pursuing, learning, and sharing with the other person fades.

There has to be a better way. Men and women can surely find ways to keep the communication lines open after marriage. During the first year in particular, they can guard against the "silence trap" which foils so many marriage relationships.

The element of the communication process to be highlighted in this chapter is the most difficult one: listening. Some experts in communication insist that most of us listen at only about 25 percent efficiency. In marriage, the percentage may be even lower still.

Dr. William Haney tells about a man whose car had

stalled due to a dead battery. A passing motorist agreed to help him get started. "Since my car has an automatic transmission," he explained, "you'll have to get up to 30 to 35 miles per hour to get me started." The modern Good Samaritan nodded and walked to his car. After a few minutes of waiting for him to line up his car behind him, the man began to wonder where his would-be helper had gone. Suddenly he spotted him in his rear-view mirror – bearing down on him at 30 to 35 miles per hour!

Dr. Haney's story illustrates how serious a problem poor listening can be. The driver of the disabled car may not have made himself perfectly clear; yet the passing motorist was not really listening.

Listening is a special skill which can be cultivated with practice. Since this ability is relevant to both our relationships with God and one another, it will be considered from both perspectives.

Some Background Thoughts

God has given each of us two ears and only one mouth. Perhaps we are supposed to see a meaning in that fact which most of us appear to have missed. Most of us would be much wiser if we listened twice as much as we speak! "My dear brothers, take note of this: Everyone should be quick to listen, slow to speak, and slow to become angry" (Jas. 1:19).

To the people of his own generation, Jesus declared that this prophecy from Isaiah was being fulfilled in them: "You will be ever hearing but never understanding; you will be ever seeing but never perceiving" (Matt. 13:14). Are we sometimes guilty of the same sort of spiritual deafness and blindness in our day? Do husbands and wives sometimes fail to see what they are doing to each other through neglect or selfishness? Can we fail to hear each other's cries for love, appreciation, or help?

On the heels of quoting Isaiah and applying his words to the general populace of his time, he told his own disciples, "But blessed are your eyes because they see, and your ears because they hear" (Matt. 13:16). He then taught the Parable of the Soils (Matt. 13:18-23). The point of this familiar parable is that the difference between barrenness and fruitfulness in spiritual things lies in one's willingness to listen. Hard, stony, and preoccupied hearts cannot receive the Word of God with profit; one who really listens, however, can bear much fruit.

Jesus often closed a lesson or specific admonition with the words: "He that has ears to hear, let him hear." Each of the letters to the seven churches of Asia ends with this appeal: "He that has an ear, let him hear what the Spirit is saying to the churches."

Most of us talk too much and listen too little. A great need in our lives is restraint, waiting, and silence. "Be still, and know that I am God" (Psa. 46:10).

We need to hold our tongues and listen – with heart as well as with ears – to the things people around us are trying to say. Especially do we need to learn to listen for the things our mates – and later our children – are saying to us.

Silence Before God

Whole families, just as individuals within them, must learn to listen to the voice of God.

In all the hectic rushing around of contemporary family life, there is precious little time reserved for peaceful and silent scenes. We chatter. We turn on the stereo. We have the radio on a favorite music station. The television set is blaring in the den. There is a need to shut out all that noise occasionally and to have some of the "peace and quiet" we sometimes feel like screaming for. "Be still," he says, "and know that I am God."

God speaks to families through his Holy Word. So there should be fixed times in our daily schedules for Bible reading and prayer.

In some homes, this means a fixed devotional period – perhaps at breakfast or maybe just before going to bed. With TV, radio, and stereos silenced, two people (and, later, their children) gather to read the Bible together. In other homes, the Bible reading may be done individually and at different times during the day; then there can be a period of worship when the things read and studied earlier are shared with one another. In still other homes, the devotional period may be connected with a meal; seated at the breakfast or dinner table, they join their hearts in the worship of God.

We are a nervous and jittery people. Everyone rushes around, but most seem to be getting nowhere. Could it be because we do not know the value of being still and silent before our God? Some couples have no time for Bible study and worship with the whole church. Even more have no time for the Bible in their private life together.

"But I *don't* have time!" You have time to do anything you believe to be truly important. What is as important as making more room for God and the seeking of his will in your life? The words of God were to be talked about and learned through the family units of ancient Israel (cf. Deut. 6:6-9) Can spiritual Israel do less with its fuller revelation of God's Word in her family units?

"It's hard to find a time that works well. We're still groggy in the morning and too tired at night." (The problem of finding a good time will become even harder to deal with after there are school-age children in the house!) Experiment for a time. You will have to work to find the right circumstances for your home. Eventually you will find that family worship time has to be set as a sacred appointment which you acknowledge and keep regularly.

"I don't know how to have family worship." This is a problem which can be corrected. You can learn. Let me suggest the *components* of family worship and then specify *three important features* to observe in your devotionals.

The components of family worship are prayer, the Bible, and songs.

It is probably best to build each devotional around a theme, and a typical period of family worship might go as follows. Suppose your theme for the day is "mission work." Begin the devotional with a prayer of thanksgiving. After thanking God for each other and the blessings he is giving you through your married life, give thanks for particular missionaries you know or who are being supported by

70

your congregation. Then read an appropriate Bible passage such as Mark 16:9-20 or Acts 8:1-8. Discuss the text together. Raise the question of how you can involve your home in the work of God for sharing the gospel with the lost.

You may want to sing a song appropriate to the theme of your family worship. (When there are small children in the family, you will find that they make the best and most enthusiastic song leaders.) Finally, close the worship time with a prayer of request. Pray for the spread of the gospel; pray for missionaries by name; pray for God to raise up more men and women to go to the mission fields. Pray for your family and any particular needs you have at the moment.

If choosing a theme, a Bible text, and an appropriate song sound a bit too complex for you, try using *Power For Today*.[1] Thousands of families use this daily devotional guide to simplify their private family worship. A Bible text and short, well-written devotional articles of no more than 200 words help focus your heart on uplifting spiritual themes.

However you plan your family worship time, remember three things: (1) Keep the devotionals brief; things don't have to be long to be sacred. (2) Keep them varied in theme and format; boredom can kill any good thing. (3) Be regular about them; whether to have your devotional in the morning or at night, around the dinner table or at breakfast, is not so important as agreeing on some fixed time and keeping it.

How often have elders, preachers, and teachers tried to stir churches to love and good works through special events, new work programs, or guest speakers – only to fail in bringing about any long-term change. Maybe our efforts have been misdirected. Instead of trying to fire up whole congregations as groups, what would happen if we focused on homes? If revival begins there, it will spread through the whole body.

Families need to learn that being so busy is often the key to barrenness. If we would shut off some of the noise and distraction and allow ourselves regular periods of

71

waiting before the Lord, our lives would begin to change in noticeable ways.

Silence in Each Other's Presence

Besides learning silence before the Lord, husbands and wives also need to learn to listen to one another.

You probably remember the fad of CB radio a few years back. One psychologist suggested at the time that these communication devices were so popular because one didn't have to quit talking until he finished what he wanted to say and turned the channel over to the other person. Think how often we interrupt people to say what we think about a matter. Perhaps without even giving the other person time to finish the point he or she was trying to make, the interrupter breaks in to speak his mind on the subject. Communication is fundamentally important to marriage, and the listening end of the process is the harder and more important part of any attempt at it.

Some new husbands fall into the habit of coming home from work and immediately immersing themselves in things so that their wives cannot get their attention. There is no sinister intent here. He may be doing yard work, reading the paper, or watching the evening news. There is nothing wrong with these things – except when they are allowed to disrupt communication.

Sometimes it is the wife who creates the problem. Maybe the man comes in and starts to talk about his work or business. The woman may not be terribly interested and say, "Oh, you know I don't understand your work. Let me tell you about a piece of furniture I would like to put in our den ..." The man takes the hint and stops talking about his interests with his wife. But very few men can keep all the compartments of their lives neatly separated. Most men want their wives to be interested in what they do and like to have their wives' reactions to the personal – if not professional –aspects of it.

If both husband and wife are working, the husband is due to show some consideration for and interest in his wife's concerns that she may want to share. For him to communicate that he thinks her work insignificant or her contribution to their life unimportant by comparison to his own is to humiliate and alienate the person he loves most in the world.

Whether you have any real interest in the topic or not, listen to whatever your mate wants to talk about. Just listening to the other person communicates this much: *I am interested in you and in what is going on in your life.*

Your Communication Skills

Here is a five-point quiz which can help you analyze the quality of your conversational skills. It could serve you well in many areas of your life, but pay special attention to its implications for your marriage.

1. Do your conversations wind up still on the same subject with which they started?

2. If not, who tends to be the one who detours the conversation?

The point of these two questions is to warn against *evasion.* It is not a constructive thing to avoid difficult or painful subjects. The wise approach is to face them directly and to select a mutually acceptable strategy for meeting them.

3. Do you tend to ridicule others' views?

When an idea is presented that we do not like, a quick desire to squelch it arises within us. One of the most effective ways of killing an idea is to make fun of it. This makes the person who suggested it appear foolish and the person who shot it down look superior in his or her wisdom. It also leaves wounded feelings and intimidates the one who has suffered from the ridicule.

4. Do you tend to deny or discount others' problems when they try to talk to you about them?

The weightiness of a problem is best judged in terms of the person whose it is. For example, husbands are notoriously bad at dismissing their wives' frustrations over a domestic situation as unimportant.

5. Can you see the importance of casual conversation about "little things" with other people?

Husbands and wives who cannot talk about the trifles of a daily routine ought not be surprised that they cannot share deeply emotional experiences in a positive manner. Communication always begins with rather trifling topics and works from that point of departure to the really important ones.

Handling Disagreements Constructively

While dealing with the general theme of communication, this is likely the best place to talk about *disagreements* and *arguments*. The two words carry very different connotations, don't they? One can disagree with another without becoming ugly and offensive. In fact, from healthy disagreements can come valuable insights for the future of a relationship. But nobody makes progress in marriage through arguing.

All disagreement carries with it some degree of stress. But there are ways to keep that stress within manageable limits and to prevent a disagreement from becoming an argument.

First, fight the tendency to be defensive. Have you heard the slogan: "When two people always agree, one of them is unnecessary"? Perhaps the disagreement can point you to something you haven't thought about. It may save you from a serious mistake. So try to hear what the person is saying without being defensive of yourself. For some men, this is very difficult. They are more interested in having the final say than in accepting advice or criticism.

Second, hear what your mate is trying to tell you. Listen not only for words and their meanings but also for feelings of being hurt, rejected, or unappreciated. At the very least, give him or her a chance to verbalize everything before you speak. It may have taken a lot of courage just to raise some difficult topic, and if you close off communication too early you may do so permanently.

Third, control your temper. Nothing is to be gained by "blowing off steam" with your mate. If you want to raise a problem or disagreement, wait until you have your temper under control before doing so. You need bridges of understanding in your marriage, and harsh words only serve to build barriers of misunderstanding.

Fourth, be honest. If you see that you have been wrong or have done something – even unintentionally – which hurt your husband or wife, admit your error. Apologize for the foolish thing you did or hateful thing you said. Confess whatever contribution you have made to creating the problem at hand, and ask your mate to forgive you and pray for you.

Fifth, promise to think through everything your mate has said. Mean it, and set a time later that day or the next day when the two of you will get together again to give your calm and considered reactions to the issue at hand. In the interval, do some careful and prayerful thinking. Is he/she right? What merit is there to his/her suggestion? Is the reaction I am making going to help solve the problem, or will it just relieve my frustration and give me a sense of getting even? Is this disagreement or difficulty an opportunity for us in disguise?

Whatever you do, don't ignore the matter or try to sweep it under the rug. Even if the best solution either of you sees is an "agreement to disagree," it will have served your marriage well to have gotten all the facts and feelings of the two of you out in the open. It keeps resentment and bitterness out of the relationship. And it reaffirms your love for each other as demonstrated in your willingness to listen.

Conclusion

Many an affair has begun because the third party was a good listener. A man I knew rather well was married to a woman who made fun of his "boring old job," chattered constantly, and seemed to take pleasure in breaking in to correct him whenever he dared to speak. He had an affair with a woman in his office. She was not a "sex pot," and I don't think the man set out to seduce her or vice versa. In all the fallout from the affair, his only explanation of how it started was, "She seemed genuinely interested in me and was always attentive to what I had to say." That doesn't make what he did right, nor does it mitigate his guilt a bit. But it does help explain how it came about.

How does any romance begin? How did you and your wife come to love each other at the start? You met, and you began to talk. After you had talked a while, you realized that you enjoyed being together and could find worlds of things to talk about. You phoned, wrote, and kept on talking. That communication welded you together in love. If the process doesn't continue after marriage, the foundation of your relationship will not keep pace with the superstructure you are building on it. Neglected for too long, the foundation may collapse and bring the whole thing down.

8/ S-E-X

The word was seldom used in mixed company in my grandparents' generation. The subject was considered too private and personal to be discussed in any public setting.
Quite a reversal of attitude and behavior has taken place
since their day.

Today the word is in common use, and sexuality is the
theme of a variety of public activities – ranging from the
publication of informative and helpful Christian literature
on sex to the depicting of explicit acts of sodomy and
bestiality on movie screens. What shall we make of this
radical shift in sexual mores? What does it mean for the
art of marriage?

I am grateful that certain repressive attitudes toward
human sexuality appear to have gone by the boards. The
subject is not a "nasty" one. The old Roman Catholic attitude, which passed into Protestantism in connection with
Calvinism, is that sex is a concession to weakness and
lust. On this view, sexual expression could never be viewed
as an end in itself but only as a means to reproducing the
race. Even within the setting of marriage, then, sex was to
be tolerated but not desired, allowed for procreation but
not enjoyed for its own sake.

On the other hand, I regret very deeply that the aban-
donment of one extreme has led – as it does so often – to

the embracing of an opposite one. It appears that practically all restraints on sexual conduct have been overthrown in the minds of a certain percentage of people in the Western world.

A philosophy professor of my acquaintance recently assured his undergraduate students in ethics that there was no way by which one could say that premarital sex or homosexual conduct was morally wrong. Another has prepared a paper for publication in which he defends sex with children under certain circumstances. Statistics about illegitimate births, venereal disease, and sexual activity on college and high school campuses are widely known. Sex is the theme of movies, television, and print. Ours is a sex-oriented culture.

Marriage is no longer considered an inviolable commitment in which two persons have each other as exclusive sex partners. Under the headline "Class Tells Wife How to Cheat," a newspaper article from the Associated Press tells of a psychologist in Los Angeles who conducts workshops for married women who are having, or thinking of having, extramarital affairs. Workshop participants are advised on remembering to cover absences with excuses a husband cannot check and to resist ever confessing an affair because "a white lie is better than a black truth."[1]

Cynthia Silverman, the woman who conducts the workshops, is in her third marriage. The second lasted 16 years. She believes it lasted that long in part because she was having affairs over those years! She thinks women need the romantic adventure an affair provides. Thus her workshops stress, according to the article, "enjoyment without guilt." Yes, we've come a long way since grandma's time.

The biblical view of human sexuality lies between the two extremes which have just been identified.

Scripture certainly does not take a negative view of sex. In fact, there is no book in the world which deals with the subject of human sexuality in so direct and positive a manner. One entire book of the Bible is devoted to the presentation of sexual love in proper perspective. It sets forth a standard of sexual conduct which is the noblest and purest known to mankind.

Neither does the Bible treat sex in a casual or careless manner. It acknowledges the beauty and holiness of sexual experience but insists at the same time that it is no mere amusement for humankind. Sexuality (i.e., our basic maleness and femaleness) is expressed in many ways, and its ultimate expression by means of male-female intercourse is reserved to individuals who are legitimately married to one another.

In this chapter an attempt will be made to set out a general overview of what the Bible teaches concerning the role of sex in marriage. Toward the end, several suggestions about attitudes and behavior which will allow sexual activity in marriage to have its intended power for good will be made.

Some General Observations

God created the race male and female. When he brought the first man and woman together, he indicated that their sexual union was to be an important part of the total oneness which he desired for them. Quoting from the Old Testament record with approval, Jesus said it was the will of heaven that husband and wife be "one flesh" in marriage (Matt. 19:5; cf. Gen. 2:24).

That the physical relationship of marriage is holy to the Lord is clear from biblical texts such as this: "Marriage should be honored by all, and the marriage bed kept pure, for God will judge the adulterer and all the sexually immoral" (Heb. 13:4). The Holy Spirit has declared that sex within marriage is wholesome, beautiful, and good; he has also made it plain that sex outside marriage is degrading, ugly, and sinful. There is a vast difference between love which is expressed in marital sex and lust which is gratified through fornication.

The sexual relationship of marriage has been ordained of God as a means by which a man and woman can express their love and commitment for each other in a manner which goes beyond words. Sex is not only for the begetting of children, then, but also for the delight of two people in each other as companions and lovers.

A point which needs great emphasis in our sex-obsessed culture is that sexuality is only one aspect of any person's total personality. This means that two people whose attraction to each other involves only sexual passion will not have an adequate base from which to build love and permanence into a relationship. It also means that, while the importance of sex to a good marriage is not to be minimized, it should not be judged as all-important to it. It means that Christians ought neither to judge their sex life by nor orient it to the claims, standards, or technique manuals which a godless world has sanctioned.

First Corinthians 7:1-5

For the purposes of this chapter, attention will be focused on a single passage of Scripture. A primary goal in mind here will be to orient our thinking by biblical guidelines. So often today the subject of sex is discussed from a sociological or psychological perspective and with no regard for a biblical point of view. Our approach is designed to reverse the procedure by letting the Bible be the beginning point for what is said and the criterion for evaluating whatever contributions other sources seek to make to the discussion.

First Corinthians is structured in the following way: chapters one through six treat a number of issues Paul had learned about through Chloe's household (cf. 1 Cor. 1:11), and chapters seven through sixteen respond to a list of questions which had been put to the apostle in written form from the brethren at Corinth (cf. 1 Cor. 7:1a).

The first issue addressed in the second section of the epistle is marriage. The entire seventh chapter is devoted to questions about celibacy, divorce, widows, and related topics. Narrowing our own study within the chapter, no attempt will be made to examine all these issues.[2] The first five verses are particularly relevant to our theme, however, and they will be examined in some detail.

As background to 1 Corinthians 7:1-5, it should be observed that the issue of celibacy looms large. Corinth was such a licentious city that some Christians there were apparently urging the single life as the only safe option open to God's people in such an environment. Perhaps the ascetic teachings of some of the pagan religions at Corinth had influenced some of the people of God in that city. At any rate, Paul faces the issue squarely.

Furthermore, although some would interpret Paul's words in this text as a disparagement of marriage, such a view has to be read into the text. It will be seen that Paul consistently regards marriage as the normal state of human beings. Also, to see him berating marriage here is to set him against what he would later write in Ephesians 5:21-33.

Now let us look at each verse in our text very closely.

Verse 1. There is certainly nothing wrong with choosing a celibate life. The Lord Jesus himself did not marry. In fact, Paul could even say, *"It is good for a man not to touch a woman."* Was this a general judgment about the value of the unmarried state? Or was it a judgment about the value of the single life at a particular time and in a special set of circumstances? To be sure, Paul points out that he had chosen the celibate life for himself (v. 7a) and indicates some of the advantages of foregoing family responsibilities (vs. 32-35). Throughout the whole chapter, however, he assumes marriage to be the norm and makes it clear that his purpose is not to dissuade people from getting married (vs. 7b, 9, 28).

From the use made of the expression "it is good" at other places in this chapter (cf. vs. 1, 8, 26), it appears that Paul is offering a *practical* rather than moral judgment about the advisability of celibacy under the particular circumstance of trial which believers were facing at Corinth when he wrote this letter. So, in verse 26, his counsel is this: "I think therefore that this is good *by reason of the distress that is upon us,* namely, that it is good for a man to be as he is."

Verse 2. Over against the practical judgment of Paul about certain advantages of the single life was a *moral consideration* which was even more crucial. "But, because of fornications, let each man have his own wife, and let each woman have her own husband."

81

In a large city such as Corinth where sexual sin was commonplace, the temptations facing a single person would have been tremendous. So, in spite of whatever practical advantage Paul may have seen to the unmarried state, marriage would remain the best course for most Christians. The type of marriage assumed here is clearly monogamous marriage: "let *each man* have *his own* wife, and let *each woman* have *her own* husband."

Verse 3. Having now granted the married state to be the norm, Paul speaks of the habitual obligation to each other's sexual needs which a husband and wife must recognize and satisfy.

In view of the exaltation of asceticism among some at Corinth, this aspect of marriage must have been stressed deliberately as a direct challenge to those views. It is not unthinkable that married Christians were being influenced to hold the view that sexual intercourse was somehow unspiritual and thus should be abstained from by the faithful. Their view would have been something like this: If not celibate (i.e., unmarried) then at least restrained (i.e., self-denying in sexual life).

Such a view is wrong, for it ignores the fact that one owes something to his or her partner in marriage. The man who thought himself spiritual at Corinth by foregoing normal sexual contact with his wife was, in fact, sinning against her! "Let the husband render unto the wife her due (her conjugal rights, RSV): and likewise also the wife unto the husband." Far from being sinful, the sharing of sexual intimacies in marriage is both spiritual and obligatory.

Verse 4. This verse explains the basis for the commandment just given in the preceding lines. In Christian marriage, sex is not to be viewed as selfish self-gratification but as the meeting of the other person's needs. It is grounded not in mere *eros* (i.e., a Greek term for passion) but in *agape* (i.e., the Greek term used extensively by Christians to denote self-giving concern for another). "The wife hath not power over her own body, but the husband: and likewise also the husband hath not power over his own body, but the wife."

Neither the husband nor wife can think of self to the

82

exclusion of the other's needs. And Paul's statement here in giving the wife equal consideration with her husband would have been quite uncharacteristic of the chauvinistic spirit of the age in which he wrote.

Verse 5. Because of the mutual needs of a husband and wife for sexual intimacies and due to the strain placed on the two of them when this part of their relationship is neglected, this important element of a married couple's life must not be omitted. It is a form of fraud when one denies his or her partner these romantic experiences which are designed to bond them as one. Thus Paul writes: "Defraud ye not one the other, except it be by consent for a season, that ye may give yourselves to prayer, and may be together again, that Satan tempt you not because of your incontinency."

In other words, when there is any interruption of normal sexual activity between a husband and wife, it must be by mutual consent, for some good reason, and temporary. Paul's fear is that Satan will gain an advantage over the married person who is denied adequate sexual expression; his or her incontinency (i.e., lack of self-control) would create a vulnerability to fornication.

Some Lessons to be Drawn

From the general perspective on sexuality gained from Scripture in general and from 1 Corinthians 7 in particular, at least five conclusions appear to be justified.

First, sex is an important element in the total happiness of two people in marriage. Therefore a good sexual adjustment early in the marriage will contribute to the total physical, emotional, and spiritual balance needed to build a happy home. Sex can serve as an extra language by which two people express their love for and commitment to each other.

Second, sex is not all-important and should not be considered an acceptable foundation for a total relationship. You must respect, desire, and pursue another person as a total being before any individual part of your relationship will be satisfying.

Third, sex finds its ultimate value as an element of self-giving love in marriage. For people who understand the real beauty of sexuality, sex isn't something to "get." It is an experience to share; it is pleasure to give; it is affection, caring, and love to bestow.

Fourth, sex must not be allowed to degenerate into a manipulative tool. Bedroom intimacy is not something to be denied your partner as punishment or to be granted as a reward for giving in to your wishes. To use sexual favors this way is to be guilty of the fraud Paul spoke of and cheapens sex to a bartering tool.

Fifth, the key to successful sexual adjustment is mutual respect, tenderness, and care.

Conclusion

It is important for the newly married couple to plan time together when they will have privacy and reasonable assurance of freedom from interruption. Freed from artificial ideas of what is "good" or desirable in sexual intimacies, they should feel free to explore their own preferences and desires in relation to one another.

It is perfectly all right for the pair to believe that God wants them to have fun in their bedroom. The marriage bed is God's design and a divine gift to a man and woman who are in love.

Any sexual activity that is mutually satisfying is permissible between a husband and wife. In the privacy of their bedroom, the first obligation two people have to each other is to bring pleasure. The only thing prohibited is activity which offends, hurts, or degrades. Within those parameters, two people should find enough freedom to express themselves creatively, uniquely, and spiritually.

9/ Parenting:
The Ultimate Challenge

In Chapter Five I called attention to the *seasons* of marriage. Of the five major periods identified, three of them involve the relationship between parents and their offspring: the arrival of a child, sharing growth experiences with children, and adjusting to their departure from home. Parenting responsibilities are central to the art of being married.

Fathers and mothers are probably taking the challenge of parenting more seriously now than ever before. Books on child-rearing skills line the shelves of stores; popular magazines regularly run feature stories about parent-child relationships; television journalism devotes a great deal of its time to the same subject. Going against the trend of laissez-faire parenthood which was touted in the '60s, more men and women are becoming active participants in the shaping of values and character in their offspring.

With more working mothers than ever before in our history, fathers are becoming more directly involved in rearing their children than in previous generations. The stereotype of men providing money and women providing nurturing is giving way to more shared experiences with children. The emotional bonding with children that traditionally has been reserved for mothers has become desirable to more and more fathers. For example, a poll of 1,200 men and women conducted by the Gordon S. Black Corporation in 1984 found that more than 90 percent of the men interviewed said being a husband/father is the most satisfying role in their lives; only five percent said their work roles are the most important.[1]

Parenting really is the ultimate challenge to adult human beings. The responsibility for the physical, social, emotional, and spiritual well-being of a developing human being is both frightening and exciting. The frightening aspect of the thought has to do with the implications of failure; the exciting part involves the anticipated result of seeing one's children grow into responsible Christian adults.

Believing that you want to do the right thing by your children – or else you would not have bothered to read this book – let's think about some of the things that are necessary to the task of being an effective parent.

Taking the Time

First, parents must be willing to sacrifice time and energy to nurture their children. The Bible says that "a child left to himself brings shame to his mother" (Prov. 29:15b RSV). Growing children need a measure of independence from which to learn self-reliance and responsibility. But a child should never be left to his or her own devices. They need the firm and responsible guidance of parents. They need nurture and training.

One of the most poignant moments in the hit Broadway musical, *Fiddler On the Roof*, occurs at the wedding of Tzeitel and Motel. The parents of the bride sing, "Is this the little girl I carried? Is this the little boy at play? I don't remember growing older. When did they? When did she get to be a beauty? When did he grow to be so tall? Wasn't it yesterday when they were small?"

"Sunrise, Sunset" has been sung at many weddings and countless parents have echoed the sentiments of Tevye and Golde. "Swiftly fly the years," they say. How true!

Some parents have experienced the grief of recognizing the rapid passing of time and opportunities with their children. Caught up in the day-to-day chaos of modern life, those parents failed to appreciate the precious here and now. By hurrying their offspring toward adulthood, making them grow up too fast, and placing too much stress on academics, they missed the joy of playing with them, helping them master social skills, and unwittingly cheated them of their childhood.

It is sometimes difficult to tell the mother of pre-schoolers whose days consist of diapers, dishes, and don'ts that these times will fly by too quickly. Sleepless nights and cranky children have left her wondering if they will ever pass.

It seems especially hard to convince the father who is trying to climb the corporate ladder that time spent fishing with his sons is as valuable as time spent with a spread sheet. He knows the bills he has to pay and he knows the hours the competition works.

What many parents of our generation need to learn is the difference between *urgent* and *important* things. Deadlines impress and motivate us – and consume our time. We complete the tasks labeled "urgent" and sometimes neglect those that are merely "important."

Asked to list the most important things in our lives, most of us would unhesitatingly put family near the top. Yet when we organize our list according to time spent, family does not fare nearly so well. We find it very hard to use our time where we say our priorities are. Pushed to do the urgent, we struggle to make a living and forget to live.

No substitute exists for time spent with our children. Not money, not gifts, not a clean house, not status in the community, not even good deeds done for others can compensate for neglecting parental responsibilities. Bringing them up "in the training and instruction of the Lord" (Eph. 6:6) requires that we be there.

Moses admonished Old Testament parents to impress the commandments on their children. "Talk about them when you sit at home and when you walk along the road, when you lie down and when you get up," he said (Deut. 6:7). All that talking required a lot of time together.

It is ironic that we who helped to give our children life

are sometimes unwilling to share our time with them. Time is, after all, the stuff of which life is made. We occasionally hear parents say they would give their lives for their children. And they probably would – if called on to make one grand sacrifice. It's the minute-by-minute giving that we have trouble with at times.

Providing for Growth

Second, parents need to be sensitive to the developmental milestones in children's lives and provide adequately for their growth needs.

Having decided to bear children, parents are obligated to provide for their offspring. This begins with supplying the basic human needs – food, shelter, and clothing. "If anyone does not provide for his relatives, especially for his immediate family, he has denied the faith and is worse than an unbeliever," Paul told Timothy (1 Tim. 5:8).

Parents are obligated to do much more than this, however. Jesus, we are told, "grew in wisdom and stature, and in favor with God and man" (Luke 2:52). This pattern of four-fold growth is worthy of thought and imitation by parents today.

We record evidence of *physical growth* on a cross-stitched chart or pencil it on the door frame in the kitchen. Sitting up, crawling, and walking are dutifully written in the baby book. We try to insure physical growth with vitamins and regular visits to the pediatrician.

Intellectual development is stimulated from the crib to college. Educational toys and games are presented to the newborn. We enroll them in pre-school while we plan for college. Intelligence quotients are measured, and progress toward potential is evaluated.

Afraid of a loner or misfit, we work toward *socialization*. Play groups are organized, clubs are joined, and lessons arranged. The child's days are filled with activities.

These are worthwhile goals. We do want our children to grow up healthy, knowledgeable, emotionally strong, and well-adjusted. Despite these efforts, however, we sometimes warp our perfect children by neglecting one aspect of their growth. Parents who show considerable regard for physical, intellectual, and social growth sometimes show utter disregard for *spiritual development.* Ethics, morals, and proper relationship to God are left to the preacher and Sunday school teacher if they are attended to at all.

Parents are given the responsibility for the spiritual nourishment of their children. Paul tells fathers, "Bring them up in the training and instruction of the Lord" (Eph. 6:4). Later, he reminds mothers of the influence they have when he says to Timothy, "I have been reminded of your sincere faith, which first lived in your grandmother Lois and in your mother Eunice and, I am persuaded, now lives in you also" (2 Tim. 1:5).As we propel our children toward adulthood we would do well to remember that growth takes time. We don't harvest crops right after planting season; there comes a time when crops are "laid by" and the farmer waits and prays for rain. Neither should we hurry our children too quickly toward maturity. Parents, like the farmer, might try waiting and praying.

Children also need time in another sense. Boys and girls need time for reflection, lazing around, doing nothing, just being themselves. Ambitious parents may oversubscribe and overbook their children's time. We must seek a balance between too much and too little.

Discipline

Third, children need consistent discipline from their parents. Your sights should focus on being firm without being rigid, being a teacher without appearing to be a taskmaster. As difficult a task as discipline may be, it is a duty that must be honored both for the sake of the child and of society.

Part of the problem some people experience in this area arises from a confusion of "discipline" with "punishment." The two terms are *not* synonymous. Discipline may include punishment in various forms but is not restricted to it. Discipline is a broader term incorporating teaching or

89

training. In fact, the word shares a common origin with disciple –a learner or follower.

Rather than being an opposite of love, discipline is a function of love. It is precisely because we love that we discipline.[2]

According to the writer of Proverbs, the Lord disciplines his children because He loves them. "My son," he says, "do not despise the Lord's discipline, and do not resent his rebuke, because the Lord disciplines those he loves, as a father the son he delights in" (Prov. 3:11-12). Homes with the right mix of love and discipline produce responsible, respectful children.

If we want our children to demonstrate kindness, concern for others, and correct behavior, we must teach the proper attitudes. It is not in the genes. Children learn what they are taught. The Psalmist compared children to arrows (Psa. 127:3-5). Like arrows, they must be directed in the way we want them to go.

The Bible places the major responsibility for training squarely on the shoulders of the father (Eph.6:4). Some fathers shirk their duty, however, and expect the mother to do the work of two parents. That is not God's way.

The father-child relationship is to be molded after God's relationship with man. The writer of Hebrews makes this comparison when he says, "Endure hardship as discipline; God is treating you as sons. For what son is not disciplined by his father? ... Moreover, we have all had human fathers who disciplined us and we respected them for it. How much more should we submit to the Father of our spirits and live!" (Heb. 12:7-9). After God gave the Israelites the Law, Moses gave them a pattern for teaching it to their children. Attention has been called already in this chapter to the instructions in Deuteronomy. "These commandments that I give you today are to be upon your hearts. Impress them on your children," he said.

The Israelites were about to exchange the poverty of their wilderness wandering for the promised land. They were to become an affluent society. They would be surrounded by people worshiping other gods. Israel had already experienced periods of doubt; the temptation to forget God was likely to increase. Are things so very different 3,500 years later? The model Moses gave then, works for parents today.

This Old Testament pattern relies heavily on informal teaching. The Israelites had their periods of formal worship and instruction. Obviously, more was required. Teaching was to take place naturally and spontaneously throughout the day. Today we call these times "teachable moments." Whatever we call them, we must use them.

The rewards of discipline and training are many. A home is happier when parents are not frustrated by a lack of control. Children are more secure when they recognize the limits of correct behavior. Schools and communities fare better when authority is in place and order is restored.

If respect for authority is to be learned, it must be taught first in the home. Submission to the will of God follows more naturally if one has learned to submit to rightful authority in other relationships. If we want these blessings, we must pay the price. The Hebrew writer concludes, "No discipline seems pleasant at the time, but painful. Later, however, it produces a harvest of righteousness and peace for those who have been trained by it" (Heb. 12:11).

Role Models

Fourth, remember that children learn more from examples than from the words their parents speak.

Whether we like it or not, whether we want it or not, our children learn from our life patterns. Observation is an effective learning tool. Children notice behavior and the results of that behavior. If they like the outcome, they imitate the action.

As parents we teach when we instruct, praise, or condemn, but our teaching is not limited to the verbal. More vivid lessons are taught by our lives than our words. When words and lives contradict each other, our children believe what they see. They are likely to agree with Emerson that "What you are thunders so loudly, I can't hear what you're saying."

Harry Chapin's, "Cat's in the Cradle," is a sobering reminder of the effectiveness of our inadvertent teaching. The song tells of a father always too busy for his son. His career demanded and received all his time. Finally, at the conclusion of the song, the father has grown old and now would like to spend time with his son. The son, however, is too busy with his new job. The lonely, old man realizes, "He'd grown up just like me; My boy was just like me."

As the song demonstrates, our lessons can be positive or they can be negative. Children will work to achieve, if they've witnessed their parents labor for success. But they are not likely to be honest if they've heard us tell "little, white lies." Neither will they have respect for authority, if they know we bend the law.

Unfortunately, children are prone to copy our worst habits. What parent hasn't heard his words coming from a child's mouth or seen his facial expressions duplicated on a tiny face. If Daddy yells when he's angry, the child is likely to follow suit. If Mommy stomps her foot and points her finger, the child will mimic these actions. Sometimes, they take our faults and magnify them. Parents who are lackadaisical about church attendance may find that their grown children never attend. We teach the values we live.

Sociological studies have shown that divorce and child abuse, among other problems, run in families. Two young people are more likely to have a successful marriage if they come from stable homes. On the other hand, parents who abuse their children are frequently found to have been abused themselves. Wife beaters often come from homes where violence was routine. Parents really are role models for their children.

God showed us who and what He is, before He told us what we should be. He sent Christ so that we could see God through Him: "The Word became flesh and lived for a while among us. We have seen his glory, the glory of the one and only Son, who came from the father, full of grace and truth" (John 1:14). When Christ wanted to teach the disciples about serving others, He served. He fed the hungry and healed the sick, and told us to do likewise. We see in Christ what we are striving to become.

Children will pattern themselves after someone. As parents, we need to be role models worthy of emulation. A by-product of the Christian life is knowing that when our children follow in our footsteps, they will be on the right path.

Independence

Fifth, parents need to teach their offspring to stand on their own two feet before God and men.

Wise mothers and fathers realize that they need to be encouraging their children to accept responsibility and independence. But of all the duties of being a parent, this is probably the hardest one to accept and handle well.

Some mothers and fathers think themselves loving toward their children by sheltering them from responsibility. They honestly believe they are doing their children a favor by making practically all their decisions for them and protecting them from the consequences of their mistakes. What they do not realize is that they are creating spiritual weaklings and emotional cripples who will not be able to handle the duties of adulthood.

Someday they will grieve over the fact that their children cannot handle school or a job. Worse still, they may suffer the heartbreak of seeing their immature child marry only to ruin his own and his partner's life because of a tragic inability to act as a grown-up and independent adult in a demanding world.

It is a natural thing for a parent to want to spare his child whom he loves so dearly any and all pain. "I had a hard struggle in my life," the parent says, "and I'm going to see to it that my child has it easier." When parents with this attitude shelter and overshadow their children, they defeat their purpose of blessing them. An infant must stumble, fall, and be bruised a few times in order to learn to walk. Adolescents must stumble, fall, and be bruised a few times in order to achieve responsible adulthood.

Beyond the companionship which makes the child know he is loved, the discipline which teaches him the necessary elements of spiritual and moral duty, and role models worthy of imitation, parents cannot then go on to live their child's life for him.

You cannot think for your son or daughter; you cannot make decisions for your child. On the assumption that you have given him a Christian framework for thinking and decision-making, you must let him face life, make his own choices, and learn from his successes and failures. While you have the responsibility to forbid your child anything that would shatter and consume him, he must be permitted to make errors of judgment and inexperience out of which will come growth and maturity.

Love your child enough to avoid making him or her dependent on you. Help him develop a security and self-confidence which will enable him to stand on his own two feet.

Conclusion

Around Easter every year, thousands of baby rabbits are bought as gifts of the season. At first, when the rabbit is tiny and cute, he gets huge amounts of attention. He is not only fed and watered but is also watched, held, and petted.

Then the season passes, and often the treatment of the rabbit changes. Now he is just left in his cage, with carrots and lettuce tossed in every day. Sometimes he is finally just turned loose to let whatever will happen to him. At other times, he may even be abused or killed. What was once a charming pet turned into a nuisance for its keepers. At best the pet is tolerated; at worst it is abused or killed; it is not loved.

Are some children nothing more to their parents than Easter bunnies are to some heartless people? When they are tiny and cute, they are fussed over and made the center of attention. As they begin to grow up, they become nuisances in the way. They are still fed and watered, but they are not loved. Yes, some parents turn on their children in physical abuse. Many, many more, however, just tolerate their children until they can be turned loose on their own.

There has to be a better way. It is the way of loving and responsible parenthood.

10/ Avoiding the Pitfalls

Marriage is a God-created and God-approved relationship between two persons. It is based on the experience of covenanting and is bounded by the will of God. It holds unlimited opportunities and imposes serious responsibilities. It is a formal promise between a man and woman which makes of them (and any children they bring into the world) a family. It is crucial that those of us who are married make those marriages work.

For the two adult partners in a marriage, their success or failure in the relationship holds their *integrity* at stake. When a man and woman marry, each pledges fidelity to the other "for better or for worse, for richer or for poorer, in sickness or in health – so long as we both shall live." To fail to keep this unconditional commitment to another human being is to acknowledge a colossal omission in keeping one's word and living up to moral obligations. Call marriage a "contract" if you will, but it is intended to be a contract without loopholes. For one to fail in this commitment is to abandon such virtues as fidelity, loyalty, and performance of obligations.

For any children involved in a home, the very *stability of their lives* is at stake in its success or failure. The personalities of children are like barometers; they change in direct relationship to the atmosphere of the home en-

95

vironment in which they live. A perceptive teacher, for example, can almost always spot the child who is from a successful home by his or her self-esteem and ability to function academically and socially; that same teacher can spot the child from a failing home by his or her inability to negotiate the responsibilities of school life. The tragic thing about battles which rage between adults is that their children are absolutely defenseless. The children suffer most and will be forced to bear permanent scars because of the unhappiness fostered in their home.

Marriage is also of *great importance to God.* In choosing an appropriate figure to represent Christ's relationship to the church, heaven chose the analogy of the husband-wife relationship. "Husbands, love your wives, even as Christ also loved the church, and gave himself up for it" (Eph. 5:25). When a marriage fails, all the parties concerned have a diminished ability to appreciate what should have been a beautiful and enlightening figure of Christ's love for the church.

There Are Pitfalls

Some couples don't make it "until death do us part." Their marriage dies before they do. Problems come, love fails, and marriages fall apart. As important as marriage is to all concerned, it would be wise to try to figure out why failures occur and how those of us still married can avoid the mistakes that destroy loving relationships.

No rational person would walk through a mine field with his eyes closed. Neither should people marry without being aware of the *pitfalls* which lie ahead for their relationship. An old adage has it that "to be forewarned is to be forearmed." Believing there is wisdom in this claim, you stand to do better in your marriage by being aware of some of the common pitfalls which hurt people.

While no list of "marital pitfalls" could be exhaustive, the four identified in this chapter are among the most common and the most dangerous. Each of them is found on practically any list of marital problems given by marriage counselors, psychologists, or sociologists.

Let's look at each one briefly. Our goal will be not only to identify the nature of each trap but to offer constructive advice about avoiding or – if it is too late for that – escaping it.

Money

Money problems rank near the top of any list of marital difficulties. It is impossible to know just how many of the million or so divorces granted annually in this country are caused by dollar dilemmas. We do know, however, that for many couples the vows should read "till *debt* do us part."

Perhaps the culprit isn't money, however, or even the lack of it. Perhaps the real problem is misplaced priorities. Money is, after all, a necessity of life, and making a living is required. Those who don't provide for their own are worse than infidels according to Paul (1 Tim. 5:8).

Money doesn't have to be a point of contention. It is a resource given us by God. We are expected to administer it wisely. Viewed in this light, it can be a "good and perfect gift" sent to us from God (Jas. 1:17).

A recent Gallup poll indicates that Americans are beginning to realize the relative worth of material and spiritual things. Nearly three-fourths of those polled indicated they would like to see less emphasis on money, and 76 percent wanted to see a greater role for religion in people's lives. As a nation, we say we value a good family life and self-respect more than a high income, material possessions, or status. Eighty-two percent considered a good family life to be "very important" while only 39 percent named material possessions, 37 percent a high income, and 22 percent social recognition.

The apostle Paul advised Timothy: "But if we have food and clothing, we will be content with that. People who want to get rich fall into temptation and a trap and into many foolish and harmful desires that plunge men into ruin and destruction. For the love of money is a root of all kinds of evil. Some people, eager for money, have wandered from the faith and pierced themselves with many griefs" (1 Tim. 6:8-10).

"Eager for money" may be the key expression in this text. That attitude toward money was a trap the great apostle had learned to avoid. He told the Philippians he had "learned to be content whatever the circumstances." He wrote: "I know what it is to be in need, and I know what it is to have plenty. I have learned the secret of being content in any and every situation, whether well-fed or hungry, whether living in plenty or in want" (Phil. 4:11-12).

Paul could live with or he could live without. "Having" was not the mainstay of his existence. It was not the factor which determined his worth. In our culture, the opposite is sometimes true. The ability to acquire money is a popular gauge of a man or woman's stature.

The Old Testament book of Proverbs counsels: "Do not wear yourself out to get rich; have the wisdom to show restraint. Cast but a glance at riches, and they are gone, for they will surely sprout wings and fly off to the sky like an eagle" (Prov. 23:4-5). And the New Testament contains these words from Jesus: "Lay up treasure in heaven" (Matt. 6:20).

With a healthier attitude toward money and things, taking another person "for richer or for poorer" takes on new depths of meaning.

Infidelity

There is no deeper pit one can fall into than marital infidelity. Of all the things that spawn disaster, divorce, and depression, this trap has the power to make quick work of its victims.

"And unto thee I do pledge my troth." Years ago, these words were included in most marriage ceremonies. I'm not sure they are anymore. The idea of troth (i.e., fidelity, good faith) has become almost as archaic as the word itself. A binding commitment is embodied in the word. A man and a woman go to the altar and promise to build a life together based on mutual trust. That trust binds those two individuals together, regardless of time and circumstance.

Troth is more than "forgotten words and ink stains that

have dried upon some line." It is a solemn pledge to be faithful for a lifetime. Those who advocate omitting the vows of matrimony and – in the words of a song from only a few years back – leaving your "sleeping bag rolled up and stashed behind the couch" don't think commitment and fidelity are necessary to good relationships. In their view of things, love is somehow supposed to be more valuable if promises are not made. The lover is not "shackled" by vows. Trust, however, is not bondage; it is commitment freely given.

The perfect husband-wife relationship is described in Ephesians 5 when Paul uses it as an analogy for Christ's relationship with the church. Christ is committed to his church without reservation. "I will be with you always," he says, "even to the end of time" (Matt. 28:20). The church isn't perfect; it makes mistakes; but these mistakes do not negate Christ's love for us. Likewise, when we marry, we commit ourselves to love despite imperfections.

Husbands are to love their wives as their own bodies – just as Christ loved the church (Eph. 5:29). He sacrificed his life for his spiritual bride. Husbands who do not love their wives in this manner do not maintain the trust placed in them.

In a similar way, wives are told to submit to the leadership of their husbands just as the church submits to the authority of Christ (Eph. 5:22-24). Wives who undermine their husband's leadership become unworthy of the trust bestowed on them.

Sexual intimacy between a man and woman is God-approved only within the context of marriage. The "one flesh" union is a privilege given a husband and wife, and it is to be shared with no other person. The uniqueness of the marriage relationship is epitomized in the fidelity of this sexual union.

The Ten Commandments made sexual fidelity the law for God's old covenant community. "Thou shalt not commit adultery," it says. The Old Testament even required the death penalty for flagrant infidelity (Deut. 22:22). In other cases, it was the one sufficient cause for divorce (Deut. 24:1-4; cf. Matt. 5:31-32).

God's plan is for one man and one woman to "forsake all others" and live one life together. We can understand true devotion and committed love by studying God's love for his people and Christ's love for the church. By following this example of faithful trust, we can fulfill the promises we make on our wedding day.

Selfishness

Another yawning pit which destroys marital relationships is selfishness.

It takes no Solomon to see that when two become one, each of the original two will have to do some giving up. What has to go – from both partners – is selfishness. Rather than "what I want" and "doing things my way," the common good must become the common goal.

Paul's classic description of love in 1 Corinthians 13 includes this message: "Love does not insist on its own way." Love allows us to give in, step back, take second place. Self-interest is subordinated to another's interest.

One gauge of a successful marriage is how many of the partner's needs are being met. Meeting needs requires sensitivity and a willingness to do for another – both difficult endeavors for the selfish individual.

Meeting needs may range from giving a hand in the kitchen to providing a shoulder to lean on. The Bible advises us to treat others as we'd like to be treated (Matt. 7:12). The Golden Rule is one of the first verses we learn to say and one of the last we learn to practice. It is sad but true that sometimes it's easier to follow this commandment when dealing with a friend than when dealing with one's mate.

In many ways, Christianity is a religion of paradoxes. When we give, we get. We die in order to live. And in order to lead, we must serve.

Leadership is earned by serving. When the mother of James and John came to Jesus seeking a place of honor for her two sons, Jesus pointed out this truth: "Whoever wants to become great among you must be your servant, and whoever wants to be first must be your slave." He then cited his own experience as the chief example of this truth: "Just as the Son of Man did not come to be served, but to serve, and to give his life as a ransom for many" (Matt. 20:26-28). Later in his ministry, Jesus gave the disciples an object lesson in service when he girded himself with a towel and washed their feet (John 13:1-17).

Paul told the Philippians, "Your attitude should be the same as that of Christ Jesus: who being in very nature God did not consider equality with God something to be grasped, but made himself nothing ..." (Phil. 2:5-8).

No better place exists for the learning and practice of servanthood than the home. Wives are asked to submit to their husbands "as to the Lord" (Eph. 5:22). The husband is made the head of the household, but his leadership is earned through service (Eph. 5:23-27).

O Divine Master, grant that I may not so much seek
To be consoled as to console
To be understood as to understand,
To be loved as to love,
For it is in giving that we receive;
It is in pardoning that we are pardoned;
It is in dying that we are born to eternal life.

–Francis of Assisi

Lack of Communication

Poor communication between a man and woman is likely responsible for more marital failures than any other single factor. Even though Chapter Seven of this book was devoted to the encouragement of communication skills, a list of primary pitfalls to marital stability could not fail to stress again the importance of sharing in marriage.

A past president of the American Association of Marriage Counselors, David Mace, says, "Poor communication is the main problem in 86 percent of all troubled marriages." From the popular press, newspaper columnist Ann Landers says, "The most important single ingredient in a marriage is the ability to communicate."

From creation God recognized "it is not good for man

to be alone" (Gen. 2:18). He created a person to share Adam's world – to interact with him, to communicate with him. God provided the perfect being to fill the emptiness in man's aloneness. Yet we often see a husband and wife who inhabit the same house but live in different worlds. God must have been talking about more than physical proximity. People need interaction with other people. Communication is the lifeblood of a marriage. When partners cease to talk, love dies.

The Bible recognizes the power of words. Solomon says that the tongue has the power of life and death (Prov. 18:21). "Reckless words pierce like a sword," he affirms (Prov. 12:18). On the other hand, "Pleasant words are a honeycomb, sweet to the soul and healing to the bones" (Prov. 16:24).

Communication, however, is more than talk. It is touch – a hand held, a shoulder patted, a caress given. It is also tone. Sometimes it's not what we say but how we say it. Communication may also be silence, ranging from the comfortable silence when words aren't needed to the cold silence when words aren't welcomed.

Communication requires listening as well as talking. The word "hear" appears more than 1300 times in the Bible. Jesus listened when people talked to him and advised those who would follow him, "He who has ears, let him hear ..." (Matt. 13:9). Proverbs says: "He who answers before listening – that is his folly and his shame" (Prov. 18:13). James advises: "Everyone should be quick to listen, slow to speak and slow to become angry" (Jas. 1:19).

Communication requires time, effort, and confidence. Finding *time* to talk and listen is sometimes difficult, particularly for the husband and wife who are also in the throes of parenthood. It is necessary, however, if they are not to awaken someday to find themselves married to strangers. Good communication is not easy; some couples may have to make the *effort* to learn conversation skills. Finally, *confidence* is required if communication is to go beyond the superficial. Talking about hopes, fears, and feelings allows couples to know each other, but it can also be risky business. Revealing ourselves leaves us vulnerable to terrible hurt. We must feel confident that our partners can hear whatever we have to tell and love us anyway. One must be able to trust that companion not to inflict pain.

Here is some good counsel about communication within the spiritual family of God (i.e., the church) which can be applied to our separate family communities. "Each of you," Paul says, "must put off falsehood and speak truthfully." He continues, "Do not let the sun go down while you are still angry" (Eph. 4:25-26). Later in the same chapter he writes: "Do not let unwholesome talk come out of your mouths, but only what is helpful for building others up according to their needs, that it may benefit those who listen" (Eph. 4:29). Then, finally, he says: "Get rid of all bitterness, rage and anger, brawling and slander, along with every form of malice. Be kind and compassionate to one another, forgiving each other, just as in Christ God forgave you" (Eph. 4:31-32).

That about sums it up. Speak truth. Settle arguments quickly. Say things that will build up. Consider needs. Get rid of malice. Be kind and compassionate.

God's instructions for communication really work. It was he who originally realized we should not be alone.

Conclusion

Your family doesn't have to be a statistic in the long lists of failed marriages. You can be in the group where only one of 400 marriages fails. That group has overpowering odds of success! It's the group of families in which both husband and wife are dedicated Christians and the family engages in regular Bible study and prayer.

With the pitfalls to success in marriage identified and avoided, you are halfway up the mountain to a peak experience. With Christ at the center of your relationship and with you family's activities revolving around him and his church, you scale the heights and breathe the rarified air of genuine success in marriage.

11/ Second Thoughts on Divorce

The very word is frightening to me: *divorce*. The trauma of the experience is second only to death. Some friends of mine have gone through the nightmare of having a marriage break down, have called in attorneys, and have been declared divorced in court. For some of them, I think the experience was worse than it would have been to lose that mate to death.

The divorce rate is in a period of decline as this book is being written. Perhaps people have begun to realize that legal dissolution solves nothing and are working out problems they might have run from a few years back. Recent popular films such as *Kramer vs. Kramer* drive home the point that there are no winners when a marriage fails – only losers.

Yet no one seriously believes that the divorce problem is about to be resolved – that divorce is about to disappear. There were well over a million divorces in 1984, and there are currently about 12 million children under the age of 18 whose parents are divorced. One-third of the nation's children live in homes without at least one of their biological parents.

In 1870, there was one divorce for every 33.7 marriages contracted that year; in the 1970s, the divorce rate soared to one divorce for every three marriages; before the slight downturn in 1983, the divorce rate had reached one divorce for every two marriages.[1]

Caring people weep for the pained women, frustrated men, and frightened children whose lives have been disrupted by divorce. What is your reaction to this statement about the impact of divorce on her life from a nine-year-old girl?

In a way, I thought I'd made it happen. I thought maybe I'd acted mean to my mother and my sister and I was being punished by God. So I tried to be really good by not waking mom before schooltime and getting my own breakfast and maybe God would change his mind. But it's been three years now, and I'm used to it all. Sometimes, when I make a wise with an eyelash, though, I still wish for Dad to come home.[2]

For readers of this book whose marriages are troubled or who may oneday consider divorce, let me remind you of some biblical facts and ask you to consider an alternative to divorce. It is a largely forgotten option, but it is worth asking anyone in marital trouble to consider.

Once when people were asking him questions about divorce, Jesus responded by turning the conversation to the positive theme of marriage as it ought to be. Paraphrasing his words, Jesus said in effect: "Let's not talk about divorce. Let's talk about God's original intentions for marriage. He wants one man and one woman to be united for life; he wants them to live not as two separate individuals but as one. He blesses the marriage relationship as the means of joining two lives into one. And he does not want mankind tampering with and spoiling that purpose through divorce" (Matt. 19:1-9).

His approach is the one I want to take in this chapter. There are as many complicated questions that can be asked about divorce and remarriage as there are minds to conceive them. Trying to answer them is like attempting to unscramble eggs and is often pointless. I certainly don't claim to be able to answer all the questions being debated among Christians over this thorny issue. That is not my goal here. From Scripture, sociological data, psychological research, and personal experience, I will be appealing for you to see the importance of making marriage work.

Taking Divorce Too Lightly

As one reflects on the scary statistics already cited in this chapter about the frequency of divorce, **he is forced to wonder how serious the commitment is in marriages.** Do most people really intend to live together "until death shall separate us"? Or have many in our day determined to stay married only "until it becomes a hassle"? There does appear to be justification for wondering whether couples today approach marriage with a casual, perhaps even expectant, regard for divorce.

With no-fault divorce laws in 48 of the 50 states, leaving a marriage partner is almost as easy as getting a license to have one. Paul Simon sings of "Fifty Ways to Leave Your Lover."

> You just slip out the back, Jack
> Make a new plan, Stan
> You don't need to be coy, Roy
> Just get yourself free
> Hop on the bus, Gus
> You don't need to discuss much
> Just drop off the key, Lee
> And get yourself free.[3]

Our culture takes divorce too lightly. While we make jokes about Johnny Carson's expensive divorce or Elizabeth Taylor's many trips to the wedding chapel, the Bible still says that God *hates* divorce (Mal. 2:16). In spite of our occasional pious hand-wringing over the subject, we just don't see divorce as the major tragedy God takes it to be.

Thus we speak of "civilized divorce" and have institutionalized a light-hearted attitude toward marital failure. The state may permit divorce for incompatibility, mental cruelty, and irreconcilable differences. Our culture may encourage troubled or hurting people to choose the divorce option as a way out. But one who believes in God and knows anything about Scripture knows that opting for divorce is not that simple.

Divorce in the Old Testament

The original and basic Mosaic legislation on divorce is found at Deuteronomy 24:1-4. It does not institute divorce, for it deals with it as a practice already known by the people. Neither does it approve or recommend divorce. Instead it regulates a practice which the hardness of human hearts had created.

God regulated divorce by instituting a "bill of divorcement" (ASV) or "certificate of divorce" (RSV, NIV). "When a man taketh a wife, and marrieth her, then it shall be, if she find no favor in his eyes, because he hath found some unseemly thing in her, that he shall write her a bill of divorcement, and give it in her hand, and send her out of his house" (Deut. 24:1).

This sort of regulation would serve to curb hasty divorce by requiring (1) a legitimate cause for the divorce action, (2) bringing the matter before a public body, and (3) the preparation of a legal document. The time and effort involved in these formalities, along with the possible return of the wife's dowry, serve to make one pursue such a course deliberately and upon reflection rather than in the excitement of anger.

As to the legitimate cause for a divorce action (i.e., "some unseemly thing"), debate raged for centuries. Some rabbis took a very lax view and held that anything which caused the husband inconvenience justified his getting a divorce; they held that divorce could be sought for any reason at all. Other rabbis argued that the words in question referred to sexual misconduct; they insisted that divorce should be permitted only in an instance of sexual infidelity.

Jesus injected himself into this debate and sided with the latter and stricter view. "It has been said, 'Anyone who divorces his wife must give her a certificate of divorce.' But I tell you that anyone who divorces his wife, except for marital unfaithfulness, causes her to become an adulteress, and anyone who marries the divorced woman commits adultery" (Matt. 5:31-32).

If a man did divorce his wife under these circumstances and if she then married another man, the original husband could never take her back as his wife. This was the primary thrust of the Mosaic legislation. For him to violate this stipulation would constitute adultery and be "detestable in the eyes of the Lord" (Deut. 24:4).

In the book of Hosea, there is a beautiful alternative to divorce and remarriage. With Hosea's own personal experience with an unfaithful wife as the background, the Lord portrays his feelings toward Israel. "But the more I called Israel, the further they went from me. ... I led them with cords of human kindness, with ties of love; I lifted the yoke from their neck and bent down to feed them. ... How can I give you up, Ephraim? How can I hand you over, Israel?" (Hos. 11:1-8).

Against the background of a woman having been as faithless and flagrant in sin as she could be, the Lord is weeping and saying, "In spite of all that has happened, I can't give you up!"

Throughout the book, Hosea remains willing to take back his unfaithful wife and Yahweh is eager to receive Israel to himself again. In this tender story, the truth is demonstrated that reconciliation is better for estranged marriage partners than divorce and marriage to someone else. There is a commitment worth honoring and salvaging.

Divorce in the New Testament

In the days of Jesus' earthly ministry, divorce was common in both Jewish and Roman societies. He stepped into that context and declared himself to be unalterably opposed to divorce. The most succinct statement of his view is as follows: "Anyone who divorces his wife and marries another woman commits adultery, and the man who marries a divorced woman commits adultery" (Luke 16:18). **This is the Lord's general rule about divorce.** If this were the only teaching of the New Testament on the subject, no divorced person would ever have the right of remarriage following divorce. It is an unqualified prohibition of remarriage among divorced persons.

This is not, however, the sum total of what the New Testament says on the subject. It is not even all that Jesus himself ever said on the subject. In a fuller discussion of marriage and divorce which has already been referred to in this study, **Jesus allowed one (and only one) exception to his rule.**

A group of Pharisees once put Jesus to the test by asking him about divorce. "Is it lawful for a man to divorce his wife for any and every reason?" they asked. The widely held view of the time was the more liberal interpretation of the Mosaic law which would have allowed men to divorce their wives for the most trivial of reasons. These questioners probably knew that Jesus did not share this view and were seeking to put him in an unfavorable light with those listening to him. They thought they would put the teacher from Galilee on the spot and alienate some of his followers.

Jesus wanted to talk about marriage rather than divorce. So he reminded his interrogators that God created the marriage relationship, intends it for the happiness of men and women, and does not want it tampered with (Matt. 19:4-6).

"Why then," the Pharisees insisted, "did Moses command to give a bill of divorcement, and to put her away?" (Matt. 19:7). Jesus' answer at this point was to say that Moses never required anyone to divorce his wife; he only gave a regulation designed to curb some of the abuses which hard-hearted men were heaping on marriage. "But it was not this way from the beginning," he reminded them (Matt. 19:8). God never intended for things to be this way. He never intended for marriage to be viewed as a temporary relationship or for divorce to be taken so lightly.

"I tell you that anyone who divorces his wife, except for marital unfaithfulness (fornication, ASV), and marries another woman commits adultery" (Matt. 19:9). There is the view of the Son of God on the indissolubility of marriage. It allows only one exception – as opposed to the many

110

which ancient Pharisees and modern divorce courts would accept. *If anyone puts away a marriage partner for any cause other than fornication* (i.e., illicit heterosexual or homosexual activity which violates the one-flesh nature of marriage) *and marries another, he or she is committing adultery.*

The apostle Paul taught the same thing in a letter written to Christians at Corinth. Referring back to the very teachings of Jesus we have just been reading, he said: "To the married I give this command (not I, but the Lord): A wife must not separate from her husband. But if she does, she must remain unmarried or else be reconciled to her husband. And a husband must not divorce his wife" (1 Cor. 7:10-11).

The will of God remains unchanged. Marriage is supposed to be a permanent commitment between two persons. Neither husband nor wife should ever leave the other. If something does happen which disrupts their life together and they separate, they have two options: (1) remain unmarried or (2) be reconciled. Divorce is not a third alternative. God does not allow them to find a new partner and forget the original relationship.

Paul then moves to consider the case of a Christian married to an unbeliever. The rule still holds. If the unbeliever is willing for the marriage to continue, the Christian should make no move toward disrupting the relationship (1 Cor.7:12-13). In such a case, the Christian is to feel a special sense of evangelistic responsibility to the non-Christian partner. By a godly life and, if possible, through the sharing of the Word of God, the believer becomes God's instrument to win the unbelieving mate and/or their children to salvation (1 Cor. 7:14; cf. 1 Pet. 3:1-7).

If the non-Christian not only resists the gospel but decides to terminate the marriage, the believer has no further obligation to keep the home together (1 Cor. 7:15-16). Even so, nothing is said about divorce and remarriage. The options for the people in question appear to be the same as were identified earlier in the chapter: (1) remain unmarried or (2) be reconciled.

111

Looking Toward a Solution

Divorce is no small matter. It is a major problem in society and is coming to be even more of a problem in the church. In deciding what can count as justification for divorce and who has the right to marry again, Christians must remind ourselves that our loyalty is to Christ and not Caesar. The laws of man may permit many things that the will of God does not.

Jesus Christ must be allowed to exercise his sovereignty not only over our salvation but also over our struggling marriages and troubled homes.

God hates divorce. It is eating away the very heart of our nation and culture. Its unchecked progress is making emotional cripples of a whole generation and threatens to make a spiritual shambles of the body of Christ.

Believers cannot pull back from insisting that divorce is contrary to the will of God. Only in the case of one who has been faithful to his or her marital commitment and then has been betrayed by the infidelity of a companion can we give our approval to divorce. Only the person who has been given a right to a second marriage by the Lord Jesus can be encouraged to marry again.

Those who have a scriptural right to divorce and remarry must not be impeded by the church or treated as second-class citizens. We must not be hesitant about their exercise of a right God gave them.

At the same time, the church must find a compassionate and effective way to minister to people who have been caught up in unbiblical divorces. We must not simply "write them off" and abandon them to the world. We must lovingly call them to repentance and then minister God's grace and pardon to those who respond to that call.

For the present, I want to call attention to two themes which need to be sounded loudly in this generation of confusion about saving troubled marriages from going over the brink of divorce: **promise keeping** and **forgiveness.**

The first theme has to do with *making and keeping promises*. Lewis Smedes has argued persuasively that, when we make and keep promises, we are being uniquely human and are acting in likeness to God.

Marriage is built on promises. In the context of telling us that he hates divorce, God specified one of his reasons. Divorce is a breach of faith with one's marriage partner (Mal. 2:13-16). "So guard yourself in your spirit, and do not break faith" (Mal. 2:16b).

Some woman reading this may have said to herself, "I want to get out of my marriage and start over with someone who really loves me. This dolt I married has given me reason enough to want to leave ... " But she remembers the promise she made to love him and remain with him.

Some man reading this may be thinking, "No one can possibly know how miserably unhappy I am with the woman I married, how beaten down." But he still remembers the promise he made when he married her, and he will not walk away and break faith.

Smedes writes:

> Some people still make promises and keep those they make. When they do, they help make life around them more stably human. Promise keeping is a powerful means of grace in a time when people hardly depend on each other to remember and live by their word.
>
> Some people still have ships they will not abandon, even when the ship seems to be sinking.
>
> Some people have causes they will not desert, even though the cause seems lost.
>
> Some people have loved ones they will not forsake, even though they are a pain in the neck.[4]

Don't forget the promises you have made in your marriage. You will lose self-respect in abandoning them. You will sin by walking away.

So even if it is very hard right now, don't quit. Please, don't quit!

The second theme which needs emphasis for the sake of troubled marriages is *forgiveness*.

113

Someone may be saying, "But I have a legitimate cause for divorce. My mate committed adultery, so I can divorce him/her and marry again."

Traditionally, we appear to have done a poor job of teaching at this point. By saying that divorce is permitted in one extreme instance, we seem to have left the impression that adultery requires divorce. It does not. Repentance, forgiveness, and reconciliation are themes of the Christian religion which must not be forgotten at this point in a teetering marriage.

The philandering mate who is arrogant about his or her sin, who shows no sign of remorse, or who makes it clear that he or she has no intention of breaking off an illicit love affair is one thing. But one who has an affair, realizes what a terrible sin has been committed, and wants to be forgiven can be treated differently from that individual. God forgives us freely, and we are most like him when we can find it in our hearts to forgive those who sin against us (Eph. 4:32; cf. Matt. 6:14-15).

Gary Beauchamp tells the moving story of an episode of marital infidelity and forgiveness which occurred where he preaches. With tears pouring down her cheeks, a lady came down the aisle and gave him a prepared statement she wanted read to the congregation. It said:

> For the past several months I have been unfaithful to my God and to my husband and I have not been the proper mother that God wants me to be. I have said and done many wrong things. Through my own weaknesses and selfishness I failed to allow God to be in the center of my life. I allowed Satan to enter my life and to tempt me and to deceive me. I allowed my feelings to control me and I committed adultery with someone. I sinned against my Heavenly Father, my husband and my own self.
>
> God has convicted me of how wrong I've been. I know I have grieved the Holy Spirit and I am deeply grieved by this sin in my life. I regret all the pain and suffering this has caused and will cause others. I am especially intensely hurting for my wonderful hus-

114

band and all the pain and suffering, humiliation and heartache he is enduring because of my sins. I love him with all my heart. He has proven his love for me by staying beside me through all of my trials. He has remained faithful to God, although Satan has taken every opportunity to tempt him, to cause him to give up on me, on himself and on his God. I am forever thankful to God for my loving husband.

I am here today with a penitent heart to confess my sins before this family of God's people and to ask for forgiveness from you and my God. I pray that he will cleanse me, create in me a pure heart and renew a steadfast spirit within me. I pray that my brothers and sisters in Christ Jesus will be strong enough to love, encourage and pray for me, my husband and my little children as we struggle to rebuild our lives with Christ always in the center and our focus on Him.

I am filled with Godly sorrow for grieving the Holy Spirit, for violating God's Word, for damaging God's work in my husband's life, for the injury brought to my children, and for causing any weaker Christians whom I may have had influence over to stumble. May God allow them to continue to grow and not let my sins interfere with their relationship with God.

Thank you for your love and your prayers.[5]

As that statement was being read, someone got up from the audience and walked down the aisle to sit down by the weeping sister. It was her husband! He sat beside his wife and put his arm around her. That sort of forgiveness is possible only in the spirit of Christ!

Conclusion

How many people may oneday read this chapter of *The Art of Being Married*? God only knows. And how many of them will be reading it because of the family problems they are encountering? They will be looking for pointers to a better understanding of the will of God for their marriage.

If you are one of those people, perhaps you will take

time to study and pray over the things said in this chapter. I hope you have caught a glimmer of how God's love, the power of promises kept, and the possibility of forgiveness relate to your situation.

Please, however good or bad your present marital situation is, seek the strength of God to make your marriage a beautiful testimony to his loving presence in the world.

12/ The Best is Yet to Be

Imagine that you married in your early twenties, reared your children, pursued your career, and saw your children establish families of their own. You are now a grandparent, retired, and experiencing occasional aches and pains which remind you of your mortality. For a growing percentage of our population, this is not something to imagine; it is their present reality. They are the "senior citizens" of our society – and constitute a group whose population increased twice as fast as the rest of the American population between 1960 and 1980.[1] The second-fastest-growing age group in the 1980s were those 85 and older. Only the generation of post-World War II "baby boom" children (i.e., the group aged 35 to 44) has grown faster.

When the first census was taken in America in 1790, half the people in this new country were 16 years old or younger. As recently as 1970, the median age in the United States was under 28. We Americans have always thought of ourselves as a perpetually youthful lot. But the nation has changed rapidly.

The median age in the country is now around 31 and is projected to reach 36.3 by the year 2000 and 41.6 by 2050.[2] People 65 and over represented 6.8 percent of our population in 1940 but will grow to 13.1 percent in 2000 and 41.6 percent in 2050.

117

Demographers (i.e., students of population variables) are speaking of this phenomenon as the "graying of America." Gerber products no longer can say "Babies are our business – our *only* business" because that company is now selling life insurance as well as baby food. And the TV commercials for the Pepsi generation now use models with eyeglasses and wrinkles as well as the traditional teen-aged ones.

Contrasting Attitudes Toward Aging

Some people do not appear to be accepting the reality of aging very gracefully. They waste a great deal of time, energy, and money to disguise the impact age is having on their appearance. Oh, there is nothing wrong with exercise and cosmetics; both can have a positive effect on one's self-image. But there is a happy medium somewhere between trying to be a perpetual teenager and falling apart through neglect. The inevitable cannot be avoided. Unless we die young, we all have to face the special challenge of growing old!

Some will be crushed by the onrushing years, feeling resentment and despair over their increasing age. Others will grow old gracefully, becoming mellower, wiser, and godlier as they grow older.

The book of Ecclesiastes is the melancholy brooding of an old man over a misspent life. It gives a paradigm case of the pessimistic view of old age. Solomon wrote:

Remember also your Creator in the days of your youth, before the evil days come, and the years draw nigh, when you will say, "I have no pleasure in them"; before the sun and the light and the moon and the stars are darkened and the clouds return after the rain; in the day when the keepers of the house tremble, and the strong men are bent, and the grinders cease because they are few, and those that look through the windows are dimmed, and the doors on the street are shut; when the sound of the grinding is low, and one rises up at the voice of a bird, and all the daughters of song are brought low; they are afraid also of

118

what is high, and terrors are in the way; the almond tree blossoms, the grasshopper drags itself along and desire fails; because man goes to his eternal home, and the mourners go about the streets ... Vanity of vanity, says the Preacher, all is vanity (Eccl. 12:1-5, 8 RSV).

Contrast with that dreary foreboding about aging the following positive statement from Paul: "So we do not lose heart. Though our outer nature is wasting away, our inner nature is being renewed every day. ... For we know that if the earthly tent we live in is destroyed, we have a building from God, a house not made with hands, eternal in the heavens" (2 Cor. 4:16–5:1).

On his eightieth birthday, John Quincy Adams is said to have responded to someone's question about his welfare by saying, "John Quincy Adams is well. But the house in which he lives at present is becoming dilapidated. It is tottering upon its foundation. Time and the seasons have nearly destroyed it. Its roof is pretty well worn. Its walls are much shattered, and it trembles with every wind. I think John Quincy Adams will have to move out of it soon. But he himself is quite well, quite well." I think his assessment of his own experience captures the essence of what Paul was driving at in the passage cited above.

Notice in particular that Paul attributed this positive perspective to a particular outlook on life which Christians have. He said: "We look not to the things that are seen but to the things that are unseen; for the things that are seen are transient, but the things that are unseen are eternal" (2 Cor. 4:18).

At our juncture in history, there is every reason for couples whose children are grown and gone from home to enjoy their life together, look forward to the retirement years, and grow old gracefully. The old stereotypes about aging – poor health, inadequate income, dying alone in nursing homes – are inaccurate assessments of the condition of older people generally.

Yes, age takes away some strength, speed, and agility. But it need not take away health, mental vitality, and pro-

119

ductivity. The medical care and health maintenance opportunities available to older people are keeping them much healthier than any previous generation of their age bracket. A study of 1980 census data found that people 65 and older on average had an after-tax income higher than the national average.[3] Only five percent of Americans over 65 end up in nursing homes, and more and more older people are making rich contributions to society long after the so-called "retirement age." And a recent two and one-half year study at the University of Louisville found that older people cope with stress extremely well and bounce back quickly from crisis situations.[4]

The most debilitating factor in the lives of older people centers on the death of a spouse. The larger family of children and grandchildren can help with this greatest of burdens, and so can the family of God. Even this high-stress event can be faced and handled.

As the climactic season of human experience, a Christian's life during this period can be positive and confident.

Preparing for Old Age

To grow old unafraid requires preparation. While we are young and assuming life will go on unchanged is the time we should acknowledge the life cycle and prepare for a full life. However, midlife is more often the time when one realizes the limitations of age and begins to lament personal potential yet unrealized. Then we change priorities and reallocate precious time.

One thing you can write down as certain is this: **worry won't help.**

The Bible helps us live rich lives whatever our chronological ages. One help it gives us is the admonition to stop worrying. Worry is probably one of the most devastating problems of our time.

In Britain a cliff that had been buried for centuries was unearthed by wind and rain. When the hieroglyphic writing on it was deciphered, one area was especially significant. An ancient writer had attempted to portray worry and anxiety in picture form. The picture he had chosen was that of a gigantic wolf sinking its teeth into the neck of a man. He saw worry as a monster-killer. He was correct. The English word "worry" comes from an Anglo-Saxon word meaning to strangle or to choke. A worrier, then, is one who strangles and chokes his spiritual resources.

God's promise to Christians is the same as his promise centuries ago to the Israelites: "Do not fear, for I am with you; do not be dismayed, for I am your God. I will strengthen you and help you; I will uphold you with my righteous right hand" (Isa. 41:10). Jesus promised his followers all the necessities of life, so long as they put the kingdom of God and his righteousness first in all things (Matt.6:33).

Another bit of advice the Bible gives which helps deal with aging has to do with reaching out for others. If you are lonely, you can't wait for someone to come along and rescue you. You have to be willing to make a move yourself. The truth is, **we all need supportive relationships.**

The great redwood trees of California are magnificent giants of the forest which tower as much as 300 feet in the air. You would think such tall trees would require very deep roots. Actually, redwoods have a shallow root system designed to capture all the surface moisture possible. These roots spread in all directions, and, as a result, all the roots of all the trees in a redwood grove are intertwined. They are locked together so that when the wind blows or a storm strikes, all the trees support and sustain one another. You almost never see a redwood standing alone. They need one another to survive.

Most people do, too. Our Creator knew this human need and he provided for fellowship in the church. Also called the body of Christ, the church offers both responsibility and acceptance for every person. Each member has a task to do. It may be prominent. It may be humble. But it is only when each contributes the help of his or her own task that the body of Christ functions effectively.

Just as this fellowship presents opportunities for your personal service, it allows others to minister when you suffer. Christian fellowship is giving – meeting needs; it is also receiving – allowing others to bear your burdens. Such sharing builds bonds that lock people together to sustain life and withstand storms.

Courage to Live

In one of the Apostle Paul's great prayers, he asked three things for his friends: endurance, patience, and joy (Col. 1:9-11).

Endurance does not mean sitting down and bearing things, simply bowing your head and letting the tide of events flow over. Endurance means more than the ability to bear things. It means to bear life and turn it into glory. It is a conquering spirit which no circumstance in life can defeat and which no event can vanquish. Endurance is the ability to deal triumphantly with anything that life can do to us.

Patience is the spirit that never loses longsuffering with, belief in, and hope for men. It is the quality of mind and heart which enables a person to bear unpleasantness, malice, and cruelty without bitterness.

Paul prays, then, that Christians will be people of such character that no circumstance can defeat their strength and no human opposition can defeat their love. He prays for that spirit which will never despair about any situation or person, which will refuse to grow hopeless either about things or people.

And added to all this is **joy.** Life can be more than a grim struggle with events and with people. Joy can bring a radiant and sunny-hearted attitude toward life. Christian joy is joy in any circumstance. It is easy to be joyful when things go well, but the Christian radiance is something that the shadows of life cannot quench.

A little old lady in a very small town spent much of her life in a wheelchair. Hers was a brilliant mind and an amazing faith even though she had suffered pain for years. Whenever people in that village, young or old, were in trouble, they came to her for comfort and counsel. Invariably, they went away with a new sense of victory.

She listened patiently to other people's troubles, but no one ever heard her mention her own. Now and then visitors would notice a heating pad, a hot-water bottle, some liniment, a quickly hidden drawn look, or a flicker of pain. To all she would say: "It takes courage to live." Anyone privileged to hear her pray knew the source of her courage.

Managing Your Time

When one reaches retirement, the management of time takes on a new dimension. Once the complaint may have been the lack of time and the rapid rate of its passing. Now you may find "time on your hands" and search for ways to fill your days.

You can use those additional hours for abundant living. You will, of course, need a plan.

First, you must determine a purpose. Examine your skills and interests. Then take a look at the needs of your family and friends. There may well be a need that only you can fill.

Age may force us to turn loose of certain responsibilities and challenges. However, it may also open new doors of opportunity. Growing older does not mean having to quit but it may require finding a new reason for living.

At a time when so many young couples are both working, perhaps you can do some special things in the lives of your grandchildren. You can be a primary teacher, counselor, and example to them. While not assuming all the responsibilities of being a full-time parent again yourself, your heart and residence can be open to them. When they are small, you can establish a close and loving relationship by reading to them and playing with them. As they grow older, you can remain an interested and compassionate member of that child's world.

And with so many homes ending in divorce and leaving young children or adolescents confused and hurting, you may turn out to be the principal stability in the life of some young person.

Second, develop a schedule for using all that unaccustomed time. If you do not schedule it productively, it will slip through your fingers and be wasted. Loving life and using time well go together. Benjamen

Franklin said, "Dost thou love life? Then do not squander time because it is the stuff of which life is made." Plan to do something interesting and productive with your time.

You may need to allow more time for completing some tasks than you did in younger days. We do slow down, but we don't have to stop. Directing your energy and pacing yourself is the key to productivity.

Third, diversify your interests. Too many of us see ourselves in terms of our jobs and our families only. Asked who we are, we may answer, "I'm a teacher," "I'm an accountant," or "I'm Harry's mother." Depending on family or job for a sense of identity may leave us wondering who we really are when we no longer go to the office every morning and Harry has children of his own. We do not deny these parts of ourselves, but we do need to remember that they are just that – parts of us. The whole of us encompasses many things; we are more than the jobs we do.

This is your chance to learn something new, make new friends, join a new club, start a project. The broader our range of acquaintances and activities, the less likely we are to lead a boring, lonely life.

Now that you have more time than before for certain things, everyday experiences can take on new meaning because there is time to savor them. The change of the seasons, sunrises and sunsets, a rosebud about to open – all bring special pleasure to the sensitive observer.

Maintaining Vitality

For centuries mankind has diligently followed Ponce de Leon's vain path to the Fountain of Youth. Wrinkles can be removed surgically, "age spots" camouflaged, gray hairs colored, missing hair replaced, sagging waistlines girdled. But aging continues its relentless march.

Real life is different from the fantasyland of perpetual youth. Real life has pain, heartache, sickness, old age, and death. Life is challenges – the most important being learning how to live.

Frances Tenenbaum in her book, *Over 55 is NOT Illegal*, comes right to the point: "If you are 55 years old, one-third of your life is before you. ... About one percent of all people become senile in old age, a far smaller percentage than becomes mentally ill at younger ages."

Aged persons get senile not because they deteriorate physically, but because society makes them fear old age. The myth of the aging process has become its own self-fulfilling prophecy: Society believes that old people must deteriorate physically, so we treat them as if they are helpless. The oldsters oblige by accepting the help and becoming helpless.

Modern research does not support our myths and theories of aging. Scientists have discovered that the brain is an organism with more potential than we ever make use of. Even if its functioning is substantially reduced, often more than sufficient tissue is left to function adequately.

Why are there so many older healthy persons these days? What really does cause deterioration among the aged? One word answers both questions: disease. We have more healthy older people (and more sick ones still alive) because we cure diseases better than ever before, and fewer people die of them. Disease causes most deterioration among the aged, not the process of aging.

So, most people still believe the older person behaves in "senile" ways: he fears change in his activities, he resists going out or meeting new people, he is sharp-tongued, he is suspicious, he talks too much or too little and often repeats himself, his memory fails, he does not care about his appearance or cleanliness.

Yes, these changes occur, but they are usually not physical. These symptoms are more often the reaction any person might have if he were faced with the emotional stress of a declining income, dying family and friends, helplessness, loneliness and rejection.

Dr. D. D. Stonecypher, Jr. has a principle he calls the Law of Aging: "Those functions (physical or mental) which are exercised tend to persist. Those which are not exercised tend to disappear." This principle is true at any age. If we stop any habit or activity, it is less easy for us to perform. The Law of Aging is destructive when helpers encourage the aged to stop being responsible for themselves.

We can break the Law of Aging in two ways:

1. Do not accept and thus encourage the belief that loss of responsibility should accompany advancing age.

2. Challenge the stereotypes we have attached to aging. For example, older people still feel love, and many continue to lead active, rewarding sexual lives.

That familiar line from John Donne – "No man is an island" – aptly applies to aging. Each of us must cope individually with aging and the changes it brings to our bodies. At the same time, however, aging affects families and relationships.

The Bible gives direction for our lives and meaning to the challenges aging brings to us. Long ago Moses prayed to God: "The length of our days is seventy years – or eighty, if we have strength; yet the best of them is but trouble and sorrow, for they quickly pass, and we fly away. ... Teach us to number our days aright, that we may gain a heart of wisdom" (Psa. 90:10, 12).

David declared in one of his songs: "Since my youth, O God, you have taught me, and to this day I declare your marvelous deeds. Even when I am old and gray, do not forsake me, O God, till I declare your power to the next generation, your might to all who are to come" (Psa. 71:17-18).

Usefulness in Your Family

Since this book has dealt with the theme of marriage and family, it is particularly important for something more to be said here about how older people can contribute to family life. There is a big difference between being a parent and being a **grandparent.** Some of those differences work to your advantage when handled gracefully.

When artist Norman Rockwell was illustrating *Saturday Evening Post* magazine covers in the 1930s and 40s, he often depicted grandma with gray hair fixed in a bun, dressed in gingham, whipping up muffins. Grandpa usually was portrayed in a baggy sweater, slippers, and a muffler around his neck, dozing – rimless glasses askew – in a rocking chair. It was fitting then for grandparents to stay home, basking gracefully in the sunset of their lives.

But grandparents today are anything but Norman Rockwell stereotypes. Today's grandmother may be taking aerobic exercise classes or participating in a consumers' rights movement, but chances are she still cherishes visits from her grandchildren.

Grandpa, likewise, may be running in a marathon or doing a tour of duty in the neighborhood crimewatch program, but he still wants to share his time and experience with the children of his children.

Despite new social attitudes and lifestyles, family experts agree that grandparents have a vital role as family nurturer and caretaker. Grandparents and grandchildren still meet critical needs in each others' lives.

Margaret Mead, the late anthropologist, once wrote: "Grandparents need grandchildren to keep the changing world alive for them, and grandchildren need grandparents to help them know who they are and to give them a sense of human experience."

At their best, grandparents are gentle teachers of the way life was, the way it is likely to be, thus providing an important bridge between past, present, and future.

If a tiny bottle of fragrance is left open in a room for only a few minutes, its odor can be detected in any part of that room. Influence is like that.

The greatest influence a grandparent exerts is that of personality. Near Edinburgh is a tomb of a young girl whose epitaph written by her schoolmates is one any of us might want for our own: "When she was with us, it was easier to be good." The most important gift each of us has to offer is just what we are.

The wise man said in Proverbs: "Gray hair is a crown of splendor; it is attained by a righteous life" (Prov. 16:31).

Past and Present

Change is a challenge to all ages. Change that comes into children's lives tends to be in the direction of added ability and increasing powers. Change challenges the young adult to live in the present and look to the future. In the lives of older persons, changes are in the direction of loss of power and strength. The old know that most of their lives are invested in the past.

The apostle Paul explained how he viewed life: "Forgetting the things which are behind and stretching forward to the things which are before, I press on toward the goal to win the prize for which God has called me heavenward in Christ Jesus" (Phil. 3:13-14).

The rule for this progressive man is not the rule of that which was, nor even the rule of that which is, but the rule of that which is to be.

Surely we cannot simply ignore the past. We often remember the things which are gone. It's good to recall the old scenes, the old struggles, the old triumphs.

"The past is myself ..." cried Robert Louis Stevenson. "In the past is my present fate; and in the past also is my real life." It was no shallow thinker who said: "Poor is the man who has no yesterday."

Paul does not protest the discriminating use of our past. Only the *abuse* of it. He warns to be on guard against its deadening influence. Action is impossible without forgetfulness.

"Listen only to the experience that urges you on," said one philosopher; "it is always higher than that which throws or keeps us back. Reject all counsels of the past that do not turn you toward the future."

Is your spiritual life hindered by excessive absorption in your past? Like Bunyan's Christian at the beginning of his pilgrimage, you are weighed down under a burden – the burden of past sins, past follies, past falls, miserable failures, disappointments, and mistakes. That burden will crush you. It will take the spring from your life.

The best way to redeem a wasted past is to raise yourself from it. Heal its wounds, replace its losses, repair so far as you can its broken molds.

The human challenge is to appreciate and value the good things from the past and to accept the changes of the present. Having given ourselves to ideas and causes of the past, it is not easy to replace those promotions with new habits and thoughts.

We cannot live in the past, but we can appreciate the past and understand how it is contributing to the present.

The divine challenge is to take God as a full and guiding partner to the life you are living. Don't live with resentment or bitterness toward life. Live with confidence in Christ and with joy in life.

Conclusion

A great deal in any person's life depends on his or her outlook. In some ways, all of us acknowledge this fact. For example, we do not by choice live in houses whose windows face a blank wall. We prefer a little patch of green grass or a tree or two. Even the traffic of a busy street beats staring out at a monotonous blank wall.

The human spirit has eyes, and the deadliest monotony of all is that of a soul gone dull. Life is a poor affair for the person of any age who looks out on the blind walls of earthly circumstances and has no spring green of faith, no blossoms of hope, nor fair flowers of love to see. Yet just that sort of confining outlook threatens to blind us as we grow older. People begin to feel trapped by the walls of age, decreased strength, failing health, etc. Life becomes a dull monotony. It need not happen.

The older person can contribute most to his or her own happiness and well-being by maintaining a proper outlook on life. Don't stare at life's monotonous blank walls. Keep your soul vibrant by having it look out through the windows heaven has opened for you. See the path of faith, and keep moving forward in that right way.

Notes

Introduction

[1]"Marriage, Family Comes First With Us," *USA Today*, Dec. 30, 1983, p. 1D.

Chapter One

[1]All Scripture quotations in this book are from the New International Version unless otherwise noted.

[2]Some people think they see biblical evidence for a prior marriage in Paul's life. Perhaps his conversion to Christianity involved, among other sacrifices, a wife who would not accept Jesus and who refused to be married to a "heretic" who had embraced the new faith. If this is so, it only serves to underscore the truth that those who are single by virtue of divorce (or the death of a mate) rather than personal choice also need to be ministered to by the body of Christ. They need to feel wanted, needed, and useful in the life of the church.

[3]John Naisbitt, *Megatrends* (New York: Warner Books, 1984), p. 262.

[4]"Marriage, Young-American Style," *U.S. News & World Report*, July 30, 1984, p. 12.

[5]These statistics have been taken largely from "A Portrait of America," *Newsweek*, Jan 17, 1983, pp. 20-33.

[6]E. Mansell Pattison, "Living Together: A Poor Substitute for Marriage," *Medical Aspects of Human Sexuality*, Nov. 1982, p. 87.

[7]"A good mate: 'best cure for depression'," *USA Today*, Jan. 1, 1985, pp. 1A-2A.

Chapter Two

[1]"Marriage, Young-American Style," *U.S. News & World Report*, July 30, 1984, p. 12.

[2]"Hollywood's Passion for Adulterers," *USA Today*, Nov. 23, 1984, p. 1D.

[3]*NBC Reports*, "Second Thoughts on Being Single," April 25, 1984.

[4]Tim Stafford, "Love, Sex and the Whole Person," *Campus Life*, Sept. 1983, p. 14.

Chapter Three

[1]Sandra Lee Bartky, "On Psychological Oppression," in James A. Gould, *Classic Philosophical Questions*, 4th ed. (Columbus, OH: Charles E. Merrill Pub. Co., 1982), p. 539.

Chapter Four

[1]James Dobson, *What Wives Wish Their Husbands Knew About Women* (Wheaton, IL: Tyndale House Publishers, Inc., 1975).

[2]The statistics used here and later in this chapter are taken from "Private Violence," *Time*, Sept. 5, 1983, pp. 18-29.

Chapter Five

[1]Ed Wheat, *Love Life* (Grand Rapids: Zondervan Publishing House, 1980), p. 62.

[2]Bob Greene, "A 'Fired Wife' Tells Her Story," *Nashville Banner*, Dec. 19, 1978, p. 11.

Chapter Seven

[1]Subscription information about *Power for Today* may be obtained by writing 20th Century Christian, P. O. Box 40526, Nashville, TN 37204.

Chapter Eight

[1]"Class Tells Wife How to Cheat," *Commercial Appeal* (Memphis, TN), Nov. 3, 1983, p. 14D.

[2]For an overview of the total set of issues raised in 1 Corinthians 7, see Rubel Shelly, *The (Im)Perfect Church* (Nashville: 20th Century Christian, 1983), pp. 63-75. Biblical citations through this section are generally from the American Standard Version.

Chapter Nine

[1]"Active Dads See Rewards and Snags," *USA Today*, Nov. 7, 1984, p. 3D.

[2]One of the best books for Christians to read on this topic is James Dobson, *Dare to Discipline* (Wheaton, IL: Tyndale House Publishers, 1970).

Chapter Eleven

[1]"Divorce American Style," *Newsweek*, Jan 10, 1983, p. 42.

[2]"The Children of Divorce," *Newsweek*, Feb. 11, 1980, p. 59.

[3]Paul Simon, "Fifty Ways to Leave Your Lover," from the album *Still Crazy After All These Years* (New York: Columbia Records, 1975).

[4]Lewis B. Smedes, "Controlling the Unpredictable: The Power of Promising," *Christianity Today* (Jan. 21, 1983), p. 16.

[5]Gary R. Beauchamp, *The Calm After the Storm* (Nashville: 20th Century Christian, 1983), p. 62.

Chapter Twelve

[1]"Census' Latest Count of Older Americans," *U.S. News & World Report*, Oct. 10, 1983, p. 8.

[2]"Ads No Longer Preoccupied With Youth," *Memphis Press-Scimitar*, Oct. 27, 1983, p. C6.

[3]"The Elderly: Better Off Than We Think," *U.S. News & World Report*, Aug. 29, 1983, p. 7.

[4]"Life's Stresses Don't Keep Older People Down for Long," *USA Today*, Dec. 12, 1984, p. 5D.